Come Sit with Me

Nancy brings her wealth of spiritual and life experiences to this delightful, interesting, insightful and inspiring book to brighten each day with the light of God's truth. She is a successful businesswoman, mother and grandmother, church leader and volunteer missionary. Nancy folds these life experiences into a refreshing journey through Biblical principles for everyday living. A daily reading from this devotional book will be better than an apple a day for your spiritual health.

—Dr. Anthony L. Jordan
Executive Director-Treasure
Baptist General Convention of Oklahoma

It is with great joy that I recommend the latest devotional book by Nancy Rowland, a friend and active member of our fellowship. She is a Holy Spirit filled speaker and writer who has an unusual ability to apply life situations to the deep meaning of a scripture. You will be blessed by a relevant, realistic, and refreshing style. She knows Jesus, and she desires you to know Him in a deeper way. Read this book and live this book!

—Bro. Doug Miller, Pastor
First Baptist Church, Wilburton, Ok.

Studded with scripture gems the author's spirited observations of everyday living stir both heart and mind. Her experiences as a missionary broaden her world-view of how God is at work around us. The plea of this book is to press on and experience God's presence consistently pointing us to Christ.

—Susan Sanson
International Mission Board
Missionary in Malawi, Africa

Nancy showed much leadership potential when she was a student at Heavener High School in Heavener, Oklahoma in the 1960's. The woman she is today is evidence of a goal oriented, well disciplined life. Her love for the Lord and His Word is evident in the writing of her books. You will enjoy her "down home" illustrations of our everyday world.

—Ruth Strickland
Retired Home Economics Teacher

"Come Sit With Me" by Nancy Rowland is a devotional book produced through a devoted life of commitment to the Lord. The lessons within the pages are learned through a deepening experience with God. I found the book to be practical as well as spiritual. Many of the offerings were things that will come to mind now and again to be contemplated and discussed. The format is enjoyable and easy for the reader. This has been a life and labor of love from the author.

—Elaine Littau
Author of Christian Historical/Western Fiction

I love the way in which Nancy has written "Come Sit With Me." The short stories on each page are filled with personal experiences and interesting facts to which everyone can relate. Nancy ties each story with verses in the Bible. She writes in such a way as to encourage a person to study the verses that she writes about. The array of subjects and how Nancy joins them to Scripture is inspiring and uplifting. I know that is book will be a blessing to those who read it.

—Mary Polglase
International Mission Board
Missionary in Malawi, Africa

come sit with me

To: The Adams

I invite you to come sit with me as we journey through God's Word.

Nancy Rowland

Isaiah 40:8

To Mr. Adams

I want you to have this
[illegible] as we journey
through God's hand.

[illegible]

[illegible]

NANCY ROWLAND

come sit with me

TATE PUBLISHING
AND ENTERPRISES, LLC

Come Sit With Me

Published by Tate Publishing & Enterprises, LLC
127 E. Trade Center Terrace | Mustang, Oklahoma 73064 USA
1.888.361.9473 | www.tatepublishing.com

Tate Publishing is committed to excellence in the publishing industry. The company reflects the philosophy established by the founders, based on Psalm 68:11,
"The Lord gave the word and great was the company of those who published it."

Cover design by Joel Uber
Interior design by Blake Brasor

Published in the United States of America

ISBN: 978-1-61862-978-4
1. Religion, Christian Life, Devotional
2. Religion, Christian Life, General
12.05.09

Acknowledgments

I owe a debt of gratitude to my husband who is so supportive of me in all that God leads me to do. He understands the long hours I spend writing and editing my work. His love is shown towards me each day in the way he prays for God to lead me in my writing and to use it for His honor and glory.

I am thankful for the many friends who pray for me and encourage me as I write. Thanks to those who wrote the foreword and endorsements for my book. Last, but certainly not least, I thank God for considering me worthy to be His vessel and for entrusting me with the responsibility of leading others to apply His Word to their lives daily.

Table of Contents

Foreword

Nancy Rowland's amazing energy and production have made her a standout to me. I met Nancy at the Oklahoma Ladies Retreat at the Falls Creek Conference Center in Davis, Oklahoma. In getting to know her, I was taken by her spunky spirit and passionate regard for God's Word. Over the last few years, Nancy's consistent and ever creative (Have you seen her Bible Studies in a Bag?) sharing of the Bible has grabbed the attention of many. Recently, she has given her early morning hours to writing her second book for publication. She connects the everyday (bees, baking soda), and her experiences of life with the eternal Word of God.

It is a privilege to be asked to be a small part of introducing this special devotional book. Nancy's purpose is to encourage individuals to be not so much students but appliers of the scriptures, to understand the gospel of Christ and consequently to know God. Her desire is to demonstrate and urge the readers to dig out the treasures of godly wisdom. Her autobiographical (not chronological) stories of family, friends, the farm, and life in general, teach us vivid details about her world. Always she combines the simple with the complex biblical characters or passages featuring an applicable truth. Her heart is to engage readers in obeying the Word of God.

This devotional book is a resource of some of life's smallest things—fireflies hickory nuts linked to individuals as well-known as Moses and as obscure as Achan. Then there are questions from Nancy to prompt meditation or action. The pages offer a look at the roles in which the author functions, some not unlike our own, such as daughter, wife, mother, missionary, leader, and servant. One of the most valuable parts of the devotionals, to me, is the multiple biblical characters, their qualities open for all to see as they walk through the Old or New Testament writings.

I was challenged as I read. Each devotional has a separate, distinct topic. Continually looking in the scriptures and at Nancy's comments on sins to avoid, promises to claim, attitudes to change, and examples to imitate, I am prompted in Christ-likeness.

Nancy has made a contribution to busy Christ followers by emphasizing the Great Commission on pages that can be read straight through or one devotional a day for almost three months.

What is Nancy's hope for this book? "To encourage others to spend time in God's Word, and let it speak to their hearts."

Reading Nancy's book has the potential to bring about what Charles Swindoll urges from Luke 24:29: "Let's invite Jesus into our homes, to sit at our tables, to break the bread of life, and most of all, to open our eyes."

Considering that worthy experience, I recommend Come Sit with Me to you.

One Thousand Blessings,

—Carolyn Teague
Founder and Director, INNERchange, Inc.,
Fort Worth, Texas

Hello Mudder!

No sweeter sound is heard by a mother than the voice of her child speaking to her. When I answer the phone and it is our son, Anthony, calling, he always says, "Hello Mudder." The feeling I have when my son addresses me in this way is probably similar to how people in the Bible must have felt when they heard God speak to them.

When Jesus came to the Jordan River to be baptized by John the Baptist, John said he should be the one being baptized by Jesus. However, Jesus insisted that John baptize Him. The Bible tells us that as Jesus came up out of the water, the heavens opened and the Spirit of God descended as a dove and rested on Jesus's shoulders. "And there came a voice from heaven: This is My beloved Son. I take delight in Him" (Matthew 3:17, HCSB)! How do you think Jesus felt when He heard God the Father's voice from heaven? These words were a fulfillment of the prophecy spoken by Isaiah, "This is My Servant; I strengthen Him, this is My Chosen One; I delight in Him. I have put My Spirit on Him; He will bring justice to the nations" (Isaiah 42:1, HCSB). God was recognizing Jesus as the coming Messiah. The words Jesus heard His Father speak were music to His ears.

The book of John tells us that even though Peter denied Jesus three times before His crucifixion, one of Jesus's appearances after His resurrection was to Peter. Jesus questioned Peter three times concerning his love for Him. Three times Peter had the opportunity to reaffirm his love for Jesus. "He said to him the third time, "Simon, son of John, do you love Me?" Peter was grieved because He said to him the third time, "Do you love me?" And he said to Him, "Lord, You know all things; You know that I love You." Jesus said to him, "Tend My sheep" (John 21:17, NASB). Even though it grieved Peter that Jesus continued questioning his love for Him, I am certain Peter was thankful that Jesus was still speaking to him after he had denied Him. The sound of Jesus's voice was pleasant to the ears of Peter.

Living our life in obedience to the Lord is of utmost importance. God had a specific purpose for our life when He intricately wove us together in our mother's womb. God gave the following commandment to the children of Israel, but it is also applicable to our lives today. "Jesus said to him, 'You shall love the LORD your God with all your heart, with all your soul, and with all your mind'" (Matthew 22:37, NKJV). When we have this great love for God the Father, we will allow the Holy Spirit to lead us in living a committed life to Him. The desire of our heart should be that God will be pleased with what we have done. "His lord said to him, 'Well done, good and faithful servant…'" (Matthew 25:21a, NKJV). The sound of these words spoken by our Father will be sweet to our ears.

Words gently spoken are sweet to a person's ears. It always touches my heart when I hear Anthony's voice say, "Hello Mudder." Jesus knew how important He was to God the Father when God identified Him as His Son. Even though Peter was grieved over Jesus continuing to question his love for Him, no doubt he was pleased to hear Jesus speaking to him. We will hear no sweeter words than for the Lord to tell us how pleased He is with our service to Him.

Think about some ways you can encourage others by speaking words that would be sweet to their ears. Perhaps you could speak words of encouragement to them concerning a particular situation they are in. Words spoken in kindness and with compassion are sweet to people's ears. Drop them a note sharing with them what the Bible says about their situation. If someone is grieving, share the words spoken by David in the Book of Psalm. "The LORD is near to the brokenhearted, and saves those who are crushed in spirit" (Psalm 34:18, NASB). God is pleased when you use scripture to encourage others. Be sensitive to the needs of others. You could call them on the phone to let them know you are thinking about them and praying for them. Pray with them on the phone. These words are sweet to the ears of those who need encouragement.

Signs of New Growth

After a few weeks of heavy rains, there was a lot of new growth on the shrubs in our flowerbed. Thinking about the new growth on the end of several of the branches, I contemplated whether it was wise to cut them off at this time of the year. I decided it would not damage the shrubs. I snipped off the small twigs that were evidence of new growth. Hopefully by getting rid of the extra growth, it will help the shrubs be stronger and able to endure the hot, dry weather we are having now. When we planted a vegetable garden, people told us that it was best to trim off some of the limbs of the tomato plants so they would produce more tomatoes. It was always difficult for me to do, because it seemed to me that the larger the plant, the more blooms there would be and you would logically have more tomatoes. I am limited in my understanding of tomato plants, but it seems if the plant gets too large it will take away nutrients that are needed to produce the blooms from which the tomatoes will grow.

Imagine how God the Father feels when He observes His children showing signs of new growth in their relationship to Him. When our children were babies, we were so excited when they took their first step or said their first word. We were pleased to see the progress they were making. God created us with a special plan in mind. "For I know the thoughts that I think toward you, says the Lord, thoughts of peace and not of evil, to give you a future and a hope" (Jeremiah 29:11, NKJV). God knows exactly what we need to mature spiritually and He will lead us in the way we need to go if we will follow His leading. When we mature spiritually, we will begin to produce fruit for the Lord.

The Gospel of John gives a great explanation about what God does so we will produce more fruit for Him. "I am the true vine, and My Father is the vinedresser. Every branch in me that does not bear fruit, He takes away; and every branch that bears fruit, He prunes it, that it may bear more fruit" (John 15:1-2, NASB). All believers are branches and we are connected to Jesus, the vine. As we mature in the Lord, we come to understand more about the characteristics of Jesus Christ and how we can become more like Him. We must stay connected to the vine in order to produce fruit. When we allow ourselves to get too busy doing things for the Lord rather than spending time with Him, the Father will take away some of those activities. If we are going to yield fruit for the Lord, we must spend time with Him in His Word and in prayer. I have had times in my life when the Lord has laid me flat on my back in bed in order to get me to focus on what His purpose was for my life. God had to prune away my self-centered desires. After pruning, signs of new growth will be evident and we will be excited about sharing Jesus with people we meet.

Evidence

One of the greatest joys in my life is living in the country and raising cattle to sell and have for our own meat. As I was watching a red, white-faced calf, only a couple of weeks old, it was evident that God was the master creator.

> In the beginning God created the heavens and the earth. And God made the beasts of the earth after their kind, and the cattle after their kind, and everything that creeps on the ground after its kind; and God saw that it was good.
>
> Genesis1:1, 25 (NASB)

The mama of this calf is a small, red Angus, but the father is a full-blood polled Hereford. When the calf was born, its coloring and marking was not only evidence of the cross breeding, but of the miracle of birth and the master design of the God of creation.

What a joy to watch this young calf running and bouncing around out in the pasture, seeming not to have a care in the world. It seems not to be aware of any danger whatsoever, but it is evident that the mama cow is aware of all that is going on around them. When I was taking a picture, she was watching me very closely as I tried to get up close enough to get a good picture. If the calf bounded off, she immediately followed right behind it. There was no question whose calf it was, her actions were hard evidence that the calf belonged to her.

In the book of Exodus we see more evidence of God's amazing power. Moses was pasturing his father-in-law's sheep in the wilderness close to Mount Horeb, the mountain of God. He observed a bush burning, but it was not burning up. "So Moses said, 'I must turn aside now, and see this marvelous sight, why the bush is not burned up'" (Exodus 3:3, NASB). Moses sought evidence to prove why the bush was not burning up. All of a sudden, he received the proof he was seeking. "When the LORD saw that he turned aside to look, God called to him from the midst of the bush, and said, 'Moses, Moses!' And he said, 'Here I am'" (Exodus 3:4, NASB). Again, we see God's amazing power at work .

The mama cow cautiously watched while I was trying to get a picture of the calf. It was evident that it was her calf. The coloring and marking on the face of the calf were evidence of the cross breeding that had taken place between the polled Hereford bull and the red Angus mama cow.

Moses was inquisitive concerning why the bush was burning but it was not burning up. When Moses turned aside to look, it gave God opportunity to speak to Him from the bush. This amazing act made it evident to Moses that He was in the presence of God.

What is the evidence that God is at work in your life? Make a list of some of the times God has intervened in your life to keep you from having an accident. Also, list some of the times God has made provision for you to have what you needed when there seemed to be no hope. These lists should be all the evidence you need to be convinced that God is concerned about every aspect of your life.

Determined to Love

My maternal grandmother, Mama Cordie, was an exceptional lady. She had a love for the Lord that was beyond measure. Because of her love for the Lord, she possessed a love for all people. She made no distinction between people whether rich or poor. She would literally give the shirt off her back to someone if they needed it. She found great joy in serving others, expressing her love for them in this way. It seemed she never met a person she did not like. She loved to feed people and to give graciously of what she had to them. Most of the time she had very little, but she did whatever she could to help them. Mama Cordie did not see any bad traits in people. "You shall not take vengeance, nor bear any grudge against the children of your people, but you shall love your neighbor as yourself: I am the LORD" (Leviticus 19:18, NKJV).This verse could have been Mama Cordie's life verse.

In the book of Ruth, we have a beautiful love story that unfolds between a daughter-in-law and a mother-in-law—Ruth and Naomi. After Naomi's husband and two sons died, she decided to return to her homeland of Judah. Naomi told both of her daughters-in-law to return to their mother's home, but both told her they would go with her to her people. Three different times Naomi urged them to return to their own mothers, because she knew she had nothing to offer them. Orpah decided to leave so she kissed her mother-in-law and began the journey home to her mother. Ruth clung to her mother-in-law and refused to leave. Ruth's words to Naomi are a beautiful picture of the love of one person for another and her pledge to the true God that Naomi worshipped.

> And Ruth said, "Urge me not to leave you or to turn back from following you; for where you go I will go, and where you lodge I will lodge. Your people shall be my people and your God my God. Where you die I will die, and there will I be buried. The Lord do so to me, and more also, if anything but death parts me from you."
>
> Ruth 1:16-17 (AMP)

Ruth was determined to accompany Naomi to her homeland and by doing this she was showing her love and respect for her. However, her greatest declaration was that she was accepting the God of Israel.

Ruth is a great biblical example of how we are to love others and also how we are to love the Lord. When we come to know the Lord, we are to make known to others our love for Him. You must determine to love the Lord with all your heart and to love your neighbor in the same way you love yourself. "Beloved, let us love one another, for love is of God; and everyone who loves is born of God and knows God" (1 John 4:7, NKJV).My grandmother made no distinction between people. She was determined to love them and to always help them if the need arose. Ruth loved Naomi and had no desire to be parted from her. She had an example in Naomi of how one was to love another and because of Naomi she had come to know and love the one true God. Think about your life. Who sets the example for you in how you are to love one another? We can show our love to others by speaking kind words to them, letting them know we are praying for them by sending a note of encouragement and helping them when they have financial needs. These are a few ways we can show our love, but the most important thing we can do to show our love for others is to point them to Jesus. We must share with them how they can come to know Jesus and have a love relationship with Him.

Nourishment from the Lord

The egg is an amazing creation of Almighty God. When I put some eggs on to boil this morning to make egg salad sandwiches, my mind began to think about what we would do without eggs. Many times when serving in Malawi as short-term missionaries, eggs was the only protein readily available. Growing up, eggs were a staple food for breakfast. We ate them fried, scrambled and sometimes poached. People in days gone by always had chickens on the farm so they usually had plenty of eggs to eat. God created many different foods that offer nourishment to one's physical body. Food is important for a person to survive physically. People will eventually starve to death if they go without food. Jesus came to earth to be born as a human in order that He could offer to us the food that would enable us to live forever.

As Jesus taught, many ask questions because they really did not understand what He was saying. Jesus had just fed the five thousand and had withdrawn to the mountain to be alone. The disciples got in the boat and went to the other side of the sea toward Capernaum. When the people found where Jesus and the disciples were, they followed Him. They wanted to see Jesus perform other signs or miracles. They referred to the children of Israel eating the manna that came from heaven. "Jesus said to them, "I assure you: Moses didn't give you the bread from heaven, but My Father gives you the real bread from heaven. For the bread of God is the One who comes down from heaven and gives life to the world" (John 6:32-33, HCSB). The people wanted this bread.

Jesus then made a very important statement about Himself. "I am the bread of life: Jesus told them. "No one who comes to Me will ever be hungry, and no one who believes in Me will ever be thirsty again" (John 6:35, HCSB). Jesus told them that they had seen Him but yet they did not believe. He then explained to them what He meant.

> For I have come down from heaven, not to do My will, but the will of Him who sent Me. This is the will of Him who sent Me: that I should lose none of those He has given Me but should raise them up on the last day. For this is the will of My Father: that everyone who sees the Son and believes in Him may have eternal life, and I will raise him up on the last day.
>
> John 6:38-40 (HCSB)

Jesus identified himself as the living bread that came from heaven, offering to all that would partake of this bread eternal life. "I am the living bread that came down from heaven. If anyone eats of this bread he will live forever. The bread that I will give for the life of the world is My flesh" (John 6:51, HCSB). In the days ahead, Jesus would die on the cross giving His body as a sacrifice to be the payment for the sin of all the people in the world.

Eggs gave us the protein that we needed many times as we traveled overseas and when we were growing up. We were thankful for the nourishment that God provided. The greatest nourishment I have ever received was when I accepted that living bread that came down out of heaven, Jesus. Because I accepted Jesus as Savior and Lord, I have the promise that when I die or Jesus comes again, I will go to heaven to live with the Lord forever. If you have never accepted Jesus as your Savior, I invite you to do so today. Admit to the Lord that you are a sinner in need of salvation. Believe in your heart that Jesus is God's Son. He died on the cross for our sin and was raised from the dead on the third day that we might have eternal life. Confess that Jesus will be Lord of your life. If you truly want to make this decision today, you need to pray asking Jesus to forgive you of your sin and to be your Savior and Lord.

Where Are You?

When Stevie was six years old, he had fallen asleep one Sunday night in church. His Dad woke him up and told him to go get in the car. We visited with people as we left the church and when we got to the car, Stevie was not there. We looked in all the cars in the parking lot and Stevie was nowhere to be found. Doyal and I, along with many of the church members, began to search our church building and all around the outside of the church. Finally, someone found Stevie downstairs in his Sunday school classroom sound asleep on a table. We were frightened when he was lost, but so relieved when God led us to where he was. "I sought the Lord, and He answered me, and delivered me from all my fears" (Psalm 34:4, NASB).

....

Mama Cordie, my grandmother, lived with Mother the last years of her life. Mom needed to go to one of my sister's when she was ill, so I told her I would keep Mama Cordie. She was never content to stay in one place very long. She would wander in and out of the house and actually forget which door she went out and how to get back in the house. One day I was working out in our vegetable garden and she would come and go while I was there. She was gone longer than usual so I decided I would go to the house and check on her. I searched all over the house, even in the basement, and I could not find her. I walked around the outside of the house and shop calling to her, but she did not answer. I wondered how I could lose someone who was in her late eighties. I finally walked out to the carport and looked in our Lincoln and there was Mama Cordie sitting in the car in her heavy coat on a hot summer day. When she got in the car, she had accidentally hit the button to lock the door. At that time, Doyal insisted on leaving the keys in the car and we did not have an extra set in the house. Many minutes passed and I could see she was getting very warm. I was getting desperate as I was trying to get her to unlock the door when she accidentally touched the button. I was so relieved that she was safe. "The angel of the Lord encamps around those who fear Him, and rescues them" (Psalm 34:7, NASB).

....

Mary and Joseph were traveling home from Jerusalem after the Feast of the Passover. They had gone a day's journey and they began looking for Jesus thinking He was with some of the other people, but He was nowhere to be found. He had stayed behind in Jerusalem and His parents were not aware of it. They returned to Jerusalem searching for Him. I can imagine the anxiety they felt as they looked for Him. "And it came about that after three days they found Him in the temple, sitting in the midst of the teachers, both listening to them, and asking them questions" (Luke 2:46, NASB). They were amazed to see Him sitting there talking with these teachers and they began to question Him as to why He had treated them this way. "And He said to them, 'Why is it that you were looking for Me? Did you not know that I had to be in My Father's house?'" (Luke 2:49, NASB). Mary and Joseph did not understand what He had said to them, but I know they were so relieved to find Him.

When we lose someone, the best place to turn is to the Lord. He offers guidance and direction to us in every aspect of our life. Where do you turn when you go through a time of loss? What does God offer to us that no one else can give?

Headed in the Wrong Direction

The other day we rounded up our larger calves to take some to the stockyard to sell and one to the processing plant to have butchered for meat. The first two calves we ran into the cattle trailer with no problem and closed the gate on them in the front of the trailer. We then proceeded to load the other four calves. A large bull calf started down the chute with a large heifer behind him. He went into the trailer and then decided to come out. While the heifer was trying to turn around in the chute, which seemed impossible, the large bull calf escaped through a narrow hole in the chute. We were afraid the heifer was going to hurt herself, but she finally got turned around and headed back towards the loading pen. When she did, another bull calf was coming in the chute from the pen. The bull pushed by her which also appeared to be impossible, because they were both quite large. She was determined to go in the wrong direction. After we stopped her from going towards the pen, she finally turned around again in the chute and was headed in the right direction. What a relief to have the troublemaker loaded in the trailer. Fortunately, the last calf loaded easily.

The children of Israel were traveling through the wilderness toward the promised land. God instructed Moses to go to the top of Mount Sinai. While he was there, the finger of God wrote the Ten Commandments on two tablets of stone. Moses stayed gone for a long period of time and the children of Israel began to stray from following God.

> "When the people saw that Moses delayed in coming down from the mountain, they gathered around Aaron and said to him, "Come, make us a god who will go before us because this Moses, the man who brought us up from the land of Egypt—we don't know what has happened to him!"
>
> Exodus 32:1 (HCSB)

Not having the leadership ability Moses had, Aaron gave into their demands and told them to gather all the gold rings that were in the ears of their wives, sons, and daughters. All of a sudden, the Israelites were headed in the wrong direction. "He took the gold from their hands, fashioned it with an engraving tool, and made it into an image of a calf. Then they said, "Israel, this is your God, who brought you up from the land of Egypt" (Exodus 32:4, HCSB).

God told Moses to go down from the mountain because the people he brought from Egypt had become corrupt. God wanted to destroy them because of what they had done, but Moses sought the Lord's favor and God relented. But, when Moses saw what they were doing, he threw the tablets of stone to the ground breaking them in many pieces, burned the golden calf in the fire, and ground it into a powder. He then scattered it on the water and made the Israelites drink it. They had to accept the consequences of their actions.

It reminds me of the prodigal son asking his father for his part of the inheritance even though he was the younger son. He went to a distant country and squandered all that he had. He had no money to buy food and would have eaten the slop the pigs were eating if someone had offered it to him. He finally came to his senses and headed back home.

> And he got up and came to his father. But while he was still a long way off, his father saw him, and felt compassion for him, and ran and embraced him, and kissed him. And the son said to him, "Father, I have sinned against heaven and in your sight; I am no longer worthy to be called your son."
>
> Luke 15:20-21 (NASB)

The father forgave him and celebrated his homecoming. When we are going in the wrong direction in life and decide to return to God, He is waiting with open arms to welcome us back to Him.

The large heifer turned around in the loading chute and headed in the wrong direction while other calves were coming toward her. She finally turned around again and headed toward the trailer. The children of Israel went astray by having Aaron mold a golden idol for them to worship when Moses stayed gone a long time. The prodigal son headed in the wrong direction when he left home after receiving his part of the inheritance. His life fell apart and he decided he would return home seeking forgiveness.

When we allow ourselves to stray away from the Lord by choosing the way of the world, our fellowship with Him is broken and we are headed in the wrong direction. It seems things begin to fall apart. We might lose our job, run out of money and possibly lose our place of residence. We question what we should do. In the Bible, James says friendship with the world is showing hostility toward God. He gives us instruction as to what we should do. "Therefore, submit to God. But resist the Devil, and he will flee from you. Draw near to God, and He will draw near to you. Cleanse your hands, sinners, and purify your hearts, double-minded people" (James 4:7-8, HCSB)! God is waiting with open arms to receive us when we have been going in the wrong direction.

The Soothing of the Spirit through Music

My mother had a very quiet, gentle spirit. She was totally supportive of my dad, who was a Baptist preacher, but she did it in a very quiet manner. She helped him many times in the smaller churches by leading music or playing the piano. Mom enjoyed playing the piano and singing in the choir. Everything she did was in a quiet fashion. After Dad died, Mom moved to Wilburton, Oklahoma, and she began taking piano lessons. It appeared to be good therapy for her as she adjusted to being alone. Many times I would go by her house after work and as I approached the door, I could hear her playing the piano. She took lessons until she was eighty-eight years old. It brought joy and contentment to her heart and the music had a soothing effect on her spirit.

Thinking about Mom and the piano, reminds me of the story of King Saul when the Spirit of the Lord departed from him. God told Saul to go to battle against the Amalekites and he was to kill every person and all the animals. He was to destroy all that they possessed. Saul rebelled against God's instruction and spared the life of the king and the best of all of the sheep, cattle and the other animals. Because of his disobedience, God sent an evil spirit to torment King Saul. His servants searched for one who played the harp to soothe his spirit. One of the servants had seen David, the son of Jesse, playing the harp. Saul sent a message for Jesse to send David to him. "So it came about whenever the evil spirit from God came to Saul, David would take the harp and play it with his hand; and Saul would be refreshed and be well, and the evil spirit would depart from him" (1 Samuel 16:23, NASB). Music brought comfort to Mom and also to King Saul.

My mother lived a life of quiet obedience to the Lord, but God used the playing of the piano to soothe her spirit after the death of my dad. Saul's life was different than Mom's because he rebelled against the Lord and suffered the consequences. Still yet, God allowed the harp to soothe Saul's spirit and the evil spirit would leave him for a time. What soothes your spirit when things around you are disrupted? You can find solace in listening to Christian music, reading the Bible and praying for strength from the Lord. I have found that going fishing soothes my spirit. There is something soothing about baiting my hook, throwing it out in the water and sitting there quietly waiting for a fish to grab the bait. The Lord will meet you where you are and soothe your spirit if you will simply ask.

The Consequences of Our Decisions

Many times in life we are left with the task of learning to do things for ourselves. I became a widow at the age of thirty-two and was quite independent. I felt as if I could accomplish about anything I set my mind to doing , like working on my car.

Having successfully changed the oil in the car, I decided to replace the spark plugs since that had not been done since we purchased the car. This was in 1978 when spark plugs did not come already gapped; you had to set the gap yourself. Being the independent woman I believed myself to be, I thought I had set them correctly when I installed them. But when I started the engine, I could hear the engine missing and the car did not run correctly. Having only one vehicle, I had to get it fixed quickly because the school where I worked was fifteen miles away and I had my two small boys who traveled with me. Clearly the consequences of my decision to do it myself were upon me. Realizing that I was not capable of doing everything myself, I had to "bite the bullet" and admit that I did not know what I was doing. So I called one of the women who taught with me to see if her husband would be willing to help me. He agreed; I was thankful. "Strike a mocker, and the inexperienced learn a lesson; rebuke the discerning, and he gains knowledge" (Proverbs 19:25, HCSB).

Cain and Abel were the first two sons of Adam and Eve. Cain was the firstborn son.

> Now Abel became a shepherd of a flock, but Cain cultivated the land. In the course of time Cain presented some of the land's produce as an offering to the LORD. And Abel also presented an offering—some of the firstborn of his flock and their fat portions. The LORD had regard for Abel and his offering, but He did not have regard for Cain and his offering. Cain was furious, and he was downcast.
>
> Genesis 4:2b-5 (HCSB)

The Lord questioned Cain as to why he was so furious and downcast. He told him if he did what was right his offering would be accepted. Cain invited Abel to go out in the field with him and while they were there, Cain killed Abel. "Then the LORD said to Cain, "Where is your brother Abel?" "I don't know, he replied. "Am I my brother's guardian" (Genesis 4:9, HCSB)? It seems Cain did not think about what the consequences would be for his actions.

> Then He said, "What have you done? Your brother's blood cries out to Me from the ground! So now you are cursed with alienation from the ground that opened its mouth to receive your brother's blood you have shed. If you work the land, it will never again give you its yield. You will be a restless wanderer on the earth."
>
> Genesis 4:10-12 (HCSB)

The consequence for Cain murdering his brother was that if he sowed seeds in the ground, the crops would not grow. He would have nothing to show for his labor. He told the Lord that he must hide himself if he would no longer be able to sow and harvest crops from the ground. He was afraid someone would try to kill him but God assured Cain that no one would be able to kill him for what he did. Because he was jealous when God accepted Abel's offering and rejected his, he murdered his brother. He was banished from God's presence and he became a wanderer on the earth. He paid a heavy consequence for what he did. My stubbornness in believing I could do everything myself, even to changing the spark plugs in my car, had its consequences. I had to admit that it was far beyond my abilities and I had to seek help. Each of us must seek the Lord's guidance in every decision we make because we will suffer the consequences of wrong decisions. Think about times in your life when you have had to suffer consequences for your actions. What did you learn from those experiences? Write it in your journal or notebook.

My Love for My Daddy

I have many fond memories of Daddy. He was very special to me in many different ways. Daddy had great admiration for the women who surrounded him in his home—his wife and four daughters. There was never any doubt that Daddy was head of the household. He was strict as most fathers were when I was growing up, but I never doubted his love for me. Dad and I did many things together. He was one of my greatest friends. He enjoyed working outside, and being a tomboy I enjoyed the same things. I always helped him with the heavy work around the home, because I was strong for a girl. Daddy always remembered special days in our lives. We knew we were special in his sight. Because of my great love for my dad, it was not hard for me to keep the commandment; "Honor your father and your mother" (Exodus 20:12a, NASB). I did not want to disappoint my parents so I did my best to obey their rules. One day I asked them if I could go to my friend's house and they gave me their permission to go, but the last thing my father said was, "Don't ride the horse today." When I got there, my friend offered to let me ride her horse and I just couldn't resist although I knew I was being disobedient. Daddy just happened to drive up while I was on the horse. I am sure you know what happened after that. I think that was the last spanking I received because I realized the consequences of disobedience.

I loved Daddy so much that I did not want him to be disappointed in me. "A wise son hears his father's instruction..." (Proverbs 13:1a, HCSB). I think this is the same attitude we need to have in our relationship with our heavenly Father. We show our love for the Lord by our obedience.

Everywhere they went Peter and John preached about the Lord and performed many wonders. The high priest and those working with him, the Sadducees, were filled with jealousy because of the miracles the apostles were performing. They had Peter and John arrested and thrown in prison because they had been instructed not to speak about the Lord. An angel of the Lord opened the gates to the prison one night and told them to go and continue speaking about God. They were brought once again before the council and questioned as to why they were not following orders to not teach about the Lord. "But Peter and the apostles answered and said, 'We must obey God rather than men'" (Acts 5:29, NASB). Peter, John and the other apostles endured many hardships in order to preach the gospel of Jesus Christ. Even though they were disobeying the instructions of the high priest and the Sadducees, they knew they must be obedient to God.

Peter and John showed their love and respect for the Lord by their obedience to His calling on their lives. I desired to be obedient to my dad because I loved him and I did not want to disappoint him. Write in your notebook the ways you can demonstrate your love to your parents and your love for the Lord. If your parents are still alive, do something to show them how much you love them.

The Tale of an Earthworm

The earthworm, also called a Night Crawler, fascinated me when I was a child. My joy as a child was going with my Dad to some shaded place where leaves were piled up and the ground was damp to dig for worms to use for fishing bait. We would loosen the earth, break the soil up, and search for worms in the loose dirt. If we did not act quickly, the worms would burrow their way back into the soil.

The earthworm is a common worm found in moist, warm soil in many parts of the world. It is well-known bait used by fishermen. I did not know that earthworms contribute to the growth of plants. The worms help break down the humus (decaying matter in the soil). The air necessary for plant growth enters the soil through burrows the earthworm has dug in the soil. Worms are also important food for birds. We know from the scripture that God was pleased with the many things he created. "And God made the beasts of the earth after their kind, and the cattle after their kind, and everything that creeps on the ground after its kind; and God saw that it was good" (Genesis 1:25, NASB).

The way a worm reacts when you loosen the soil around it reminds me of how some Christians are in their commitment to the Lord. They surface every so often and appear for Sunday school or for a worship service. We hope this is an outward sign of their renewal of their commitment to the Lord, but the next Sunday they burrow back into their hiding place and cannot be found in worship.

In the book of Revelation, the church of Laodicea had its problems the same as we do today. The church did not see the needs within the church nor did they face the truth about their church. "I know your works, that you are neither cold nor hot. I wish that you were cold or hot. So, because you are lukewarm, and neither hot nor cold, I am going to vomit you out of My mouth" (Revelation 3:15-16, HCSB). The church is a body of believers. When the church recognizes the sin within the church and confesses it to the Lord, we will receive all that we need to accomplish God's purpose. We must recognize those characteristics found within a body of believers that are a hindrance to the effectiveness of the church.

Warren Wiersbe mentioned three spiritual temperatures in the life of a Christian, a burning heart, a cold heart, and a lukewarm heart. The lukewarm Christian is comfortable, complacent, and does not realize his need. He likes things the way they are and sees no need for change. This reminds me of those "earthworm" Christians that frequent the church every so often. There are some who come each Sunday, but never really become involved in the ministries of the church. They simply come, receive what the pastor has for them, and return home. The Bible clearly states how we need to be. "Do not lack diligence; be fervent in spirit; serve the Lord" (Romans 12:11, HCSB). Being lukewarm is distasteful to the Lord.

Studying about the earthworm, I found that they have no lungs or gills. The worm breathes through its skin, which is in contact with the air between the particles of soil. When it rains these air spaces fill with water and the worm must come to the surface or it will drown. We see those Sunday Christians surface every so often because they are drowning from a torrential downpour of problems that engulfs their lives. They seek refuge in the Lord. We consider these Christians to be lukewarm. If you are in this category, what can you do to change the temperature of your spiritual heart? First and foremost, you must spend time with the Lord daily in His word. Bible study is important to our growth as a believer. As we study and the Holy Spirit brings things to mind concerning a need in our life, we must stop and pray seeking God's direction in our lives. Secondly, it is necessary as believers that we fellowship with fellow Christians in a church setting. We are encouraged by being with other believers and hearing their testimonies about how God has met their need and brought comfort in particular situations. God has a way of bringing people together to offer encouragement to one another.

A born again believer should not be like the earthworm that has to surface every so often to breathe when the ground is wet from the rain. A person who truly has an intimate love relationship with the Lord will have a burning desire to cultivate that relationship by being taught the Bible and hearing it preached by an anointed man of God. How is the temperature of your heart? Are you hot, lukewarm or cold? Check the temperature of your heart.

The Salt of the Earth

We have a small cattle ranch on 120 acres in the country. We run a small herd of cattle on our land. My husband always keeps salt out for the cattle to have to lick. It seems that salt is a very important mineral for cattle and other animals. It is necessary for reproduction, general body health and development. We feed our cattle cubes during the winter months. The remaining eight months, our cattle graze on grass. The soil that grows the grass is normally lacking in minerals so the cattle do not get the minerals they need from the grass. In order to have healthy cattle and insure a good crop of calves from our mama cows, we keep salt out for them year round to supplement their diet.

The Bible refers to salt more than thirty times according to the encyclopedia. Abimelech came against the city of Shechem with his army and took the city. "And Abimelech fought against the city all that day, and he captured the city and killed the people who were in it; then he razed the city and sowed it with salt" (Judges 9:45, NASB). By doing this, he did not intend for the ground to be unfruitful, but it was a symbol of perpetual desolation and a sign that Shechem would never be rebuilt. If this had been forecast by God or by a prophet of God, it would have been so, but the wicked Abimelech did not have the authority to make that prediction. Shechem was later rebuilt.

Jesus used salt to illustrate a point. “Salt is good; but if the salt becomes unsalty, with what will you make it salty again? Have salt in yourselves, and be at peace with one another” (Mark 9:50, NASB). As followers of the Lord Jesus, we are to influence the world for good by living in harmony with one another. Jesus also said, “You are the salt of the earth; but if the salt has become tasteless, how will it be made salty again? It is good for nothing anymore, except to be thrown out and trampled under foot by men” (Matthew 5:13, NASB). Salt becomes tasteless when it loses its strength or its quality. When we are not walking in harmony with the Lord, we will not likely be in harmony with our fellowman. If our love relationship with God is not what it should be, we will not have a good influence on people. We must walk in step with the Lord, so other people will desire to have the same relationship with Jesus that we have. They will see the difference He makes in our life.

Salt is used many times to illustrate characteristics of the Christian life "Let your speech always be with grace, seasoned, as it were, with salt, so that you may know how you should respond to each person" (Colossians 4:6, NASB). Knowing how to respond to others when you are speaking to them is a real gift from God. We are to always be gracious when we speak to others. Our speech should encourage others in their daily life and their walk with the Lord. When we are walking in harmony with the Lord, our life will be an encouragement to others. We must be sure our speech is seasoned with salt in order that we will respond to people in the proper fashion. Jesus told the disciples and I believe He says the same to us today; "You are the salt of the earth;" (Matthew 5:13a, NASB).

Our cattle need salt in order to keep them in good condition and enable them to have healthy calves. Salt is necessary in the diet of animals and people. We need to season our speech with salt so we build people up and not tear them down when we respond to them.

The Process of Bargaining

If there is one thing I dislike, it is bargaining with salesmen about the price of a car. I would rather stay home in the quiet of our country home and let Doyal, my husband, take care of it. But, we decided it was time to look for a new car because I was traveling so much. We went to Muskogee to pick up some rebar for our concrete business and decided to stop at the place where we had purchased other cars. The salesman showed us a Mercury Mariner that had many special features that we did not have on our current car. We drove the vehicle and really liked it. Doyal began the process of bargaining with them because we knew the amount we wished to pay. He is very wise in dealing for cars and knows what type of counteroffer they should make in the process. This process went on for three hours. Doyal would refuse their offers because they were not close to the amount we had determined to spend. One time we got up and went outside to look at other vehicles. The salesman asked if we were not interested in the Mercury anymore and Doyal told him they were not making an offer that was acceptable. Finally, they asked him what they would have to do to sell us the car. He told them exactly what he expected and they finally agreed.

The sons of Israel had done much evil in the eyes of the Lord and He gave them into the hands of Midian for seven years. The Israelites would sow their crops and the Midianites would come and destroy them. They left them with no livestock and completely took over their land. The angel of the Lord approached Gideon where he was beating out wheat in the wine press. "And the angel of the LORD appeared to him and said to him, "The LORD is with you, O valiant warrior" (Judges 6:12, NASB). Gideon questioned the angel of the Lord as to why devastation was happening to Israel if the Lord was with them. "And the LORD looked at him and said, 'Go in this your strength and deliver Israel from the hand of Midian. Have I not sent you'" (Judges 6:14, NASB)? Gideon began to bargain with the Lord by asking Him for a sign that it was really the Lord speaking to him. Gideon cooked a young goat and some unleavened bread and brought it to the angel of the Lord. The angel of God had him pour out the broth from the meat and lay the meat and bread on a rock. He touched it with his staff and fire came up from the rock and consumed it. Gideon realized he had seen the face of the angel of the Lord.

Gideon destroyed the altar of Baal and the Asherah and built an altar to God. Because of Gideon's actions, the men of the city were searching for him. Gideon sent out messengers to gather men to fight. Once again, Gideon bargained with God.

> Then Gideon said to God, "If Thou wilt deliver Israel through me, as Thou hast spoken, behold, I will put a fleece of wool on the threshing floor.

> If there is dew on the fleece only, and it is dry on all the ground, then I will know that Thou wilt deliver Israel through me, as Thou hast spoken."
>
> Judges 6:36-37 (NASB)

The fleece was wet the next morning. Gideon once again bargained with God by asking Him to make the ground wet and the fleece dry. The Lord did as he asked. Gideon went to battle for the Lord and God did as He promised.

Have you ever bargained with the Lord? Many times people have bargained with God concerning a loved one that is critically ill telling God that if He will heal their family member, they will serve Him completely. Many times they do not stay true to their promise if the person is healed. God knows the true condition of the sick person and He knows what the future holds for that person. Possibly because of the person's condition they would not have a quality life. As believers, we must pray that God will do what is best for the person rather than what we desire and trust Him to do it. It is not our place to bargain with God.

How do you react when God calls you to do something you know is far beyond your ability? Sometimes God calls us to do something far beyond our capabilities and we begin to bargain with God and give all kinds of excuses as to why we cannot do what He has purposed in our life. For example, I felt this way when a friend prayed about me writing a devotional book without me knowing it. One day she called and suggested it to me that I needed to pray about using illustrations from my life to write a book. I could not believe what I was hearing and I made all kinds of excuses as to why I could not do that. We were getting ready to go to Malawi, Africa on a mission trip for about three weeks and her last words to me were; "Pray about it." I agreed to pray as I traveled and worked. A few days after returning home as I walked from my bedroom to my office, God showed me this was exactly what I was to do. Oh, what blessings I would have missed if I had continued bargaining with God concerning my lack of ability to do the task He laid before me. God proved His power to Gideon and He certainly has proven to me that with God all things are possible.

A Strong Unpleasant Odor

The other day I set a couple of mousetraps in our den. It is a large room that we seldom use, but it seems that these little creatures love to inhabit this room. This is one of the drawbacks of living in the country. The next day I went to check the traps and the one that was in view from our dining area was gone. I searched all around the room and under everything, but I did not find the trap. Finally, I asked my husband to come help me move the couch with the hide-a-bed in it. and we moved the couch. There under the couch was the trap with a mouse in it. He had scurried around the room with the trap around his body before he died. Think about what would have happened if we had not found the dead mouse. Within a short time the body hidden under our couch would have started to decay causing a strong unpleasant odor in our house.

What happens in our life when we sin, but we do not confess that sin to the Lord seeking His forgiveness? Our relationship with the Lord begins to decay because of the unconfessed sin. It causes a strong unpleasant odor that is unbearable. The stench of sin in our life is something we cannot get away from. It eats at us continually and there seems to be no way of getting away from the discomfort that it causes. The only solution to our predicament is to admit that we have sinned and confess it to the Lord. "If we confess our sins, He is faithful and righteous to forgive us our sins and to cleanse us from all unrighteousness" (1 John 1:9, HCSB). The Lord Jesus promises forgiveness to all who come to Him confessing the sin in his or her life.

David was faced with the need of forgiveness after committing adultery with Bathsheba. We find that David kept silent about his sin against Bathsheba and Uriah for quite some time. “When I kept silent, my bones grew old through my groaning all the day long. For day and night Your hand was heavy upon me; my vitality was turned into the drought of summer” (Psalm 32:3-4, NKJV). Even though others were involved in what he did, his sin was actually against God. In order to receive forgiveness of his sin, he needed to confess it to God. “I acknowledged my sin to You, and my iniquity I have not hidden. I said, ‘I will confess my transgressions to the LORD,’ and You forgave the iniquity of my sin” (Psalm 32:5, NKJV).

Mice are caught in a trap many times when they invade our home. If they are not found immediately, they will put off a very unpleasant odor as their body begins to rot. If they had not invaded our home, they might have lived a longer life.

David experienced physical pain and all life seemed to be drained from him because he did not confess his sin to the Lord. David was in anguish because his sin was like a trap around him. When sin is allowed to remain in our life, nothing pleasant comes to us or to those around us. We must seek God’s deliverance from our sin. “He who conceals his transgressions will not prosper, but he who confesses and forsakes them will find compassion" (Proverbs 28:13, NASB).

We must walk in close relationship with the Lord, clothed in the full armor of God so Satan cannot get a foothold in our life causing us to sin. When you arise each morning, you must remember to put on the full armor of God one piece at a time. If you do not, Satan will attack when you least expect it. The sin that comes into your life will trap you and as it eats away at your innermost being, it will cause decay in your attitude, actions and your overall relationship with Jesus putting off an unpleasant odor.

The Hard Shell of a Hickory Nut

God has given us an abundance of hickory nuts this year. I have probably spent at least four hours raking the hickory nuts up from two trees in our front yard. I filled our six cubic foot wheelbarrow two different times to the point of almost overflowing and hauled the nuts out in the pasture. It seemed like a never-ending task because as I raked, I heard nuts falling to the ground all around me. Our dog, Daisy, loves this time of the year. It seems she is a connoisseur of hickory nuts. While I was raking, she was lying there continually cracking nuts with her jaw teeth and chewing up the meat of the nut. I do not understand how her system digests the pieces of the hard shell that she is bound to swallow. These nuts are hard to crack with a hammer and it is amazing how Daisy can crack them so easily with her jaw teeth.

God was disturbed with the Israelites and all the nations that had rebelled against Him. The Lord spoke to Ezekiel and told him that He wanted him to go and speak His words to them. "The children are obstinate and hard-hearted. I am sending you to them, and you must say to them: This is what the Lord GOD says" (Ezekiel 2:4, HCSB). The Lord told Ezekiel to listen to what He was going to tell him and to not be rebellious like they were.

> He said to me: "Son of man, eat what you find here. Eat this scroll, then go and speak to the house of Israel." So I opened my mouth, and he fed me the scroll. "Son of man," he said to me, "eat and fill your stomach with this scroll I am giving you." So I ate it, and it was as sweet as honey in my mouth.
>
> Ezekiel 3:1-3 (HCSB)

The Bible tells us that Ezekiel ate the scroll that God gave to him and it was sweet as honey to his mouth. The Lord wanted Ezekiel to eat and digest all that He wanted him to speak to the children of Israel. God told Ezekiel that they would not want to listen to him. "But the house of Israel will not want to listen to you because they do not want to listen to Me. For the whole house of Israel is hardheaded and hardhearted" (Ezekiel 3:7, HCSB). But, God prepared Ezekiel to be able to endure their rebellion. The Lord made Ezekiel's face as hard as their faces and his forehead as hard as their foreheads. He made Ezekiel's forehead like a diamond that was harder than flint. God told Ezekiel not to be afraid of them and not to get discouraged. Ezekiel did as God said and went to these rebellious Israelites to deliver God's message to them.

The shell of a hickory nut is so hard it is difficult at times to crack them with a hammer. But, God equipped our dog with jaw teeth to crack them into tiny pieces. The children of Israel were a rebellious people and God was very disturbed with their attitude. He referred to them as being hardheaded and hard-hearted. Ezekiel would have a hard time getting them to listen to the message God gave him to deliver to them. God equipped Ezekiel with a forehead as hard as theirs because God gave him a forehead that was like a diamond, harder than flint. God wanted Ezekiel to be able to stand against them and deliver His message.

God will equip us as believers to stand strong against the attacks of Satan and the harsh attitudes of the people who are lost without Jesus. But, we must know the Word of God and be able to use it as we witness to others. "For the word of God is living and effective and sharper than any two-edged sword, penetrating as far as to divide soul, spirit, joints, and marrow; it is a judge of the ideas and thoughts of the heart" (Hebrews 4:12, HCSB). The Word of God is capable of penetrating even the hardest shell that covers the heart of a rebellious sinner.

Drought Revisited

When rains fail to come, we experience a very dry season. It is considered a time of drought if it continues for several months. We experienced this in southeast Oklahoma in 2009. The grass was so dry that it would crackle as we walked across it. The water in our ponds was evaporating and it looked green and murky. Leaves on the trees were already turning brown and yellow even though it was the first part of August. We live in an area where we are surrounded by many types of trees. The pine trees were still green at the bottom of the hill, but through the center there were other types of trees that were already brown. Across the top of the hill, there were more green pine trees. When I asked my husband about this, he said that the trees at the bottom received water from the streams or creeks. The trees across the middle of the mountain did not have access to this water and they were possibly in a type of soil that would not hold moisture. The trees at the top were probably in very rocky soil so their roots had gone down deeper and they were able to withstand dry weather.

Thinking of a drought reminds me of a scripture from the book of Psalms. "God, You are my God; I eagerly seek You. I thirst for You; my body faints for you in a land that is dry, desolate, and without water"

(Psalm 63:1, HCSB). David was in the wilderness of Judah. Canaan was considered to be a very fruitful land where the people were many. There were wilderness areas where the land was less fruitful and less inhabited. We think of the wilderness as a lonely, solitary, and desolate place.

David was out in the wilderness of Judah away from God's presence. He said he was thirsting for God, not so much because it was a wilderness, but because he was away from the ark, from the word, and the sacraments. "So I gaze on You in the sanctuary to see Your strength and Your glory" (Psalm 63:2, HCSB). In the first verse, David spoke about thirsting for the Lord. He had a deep yearning and a desire to experience the presence of the Lord in his life. In the second verse, he had a strong desire to see the Lord in His temple and to see His power and glory displayed. He was in the dry, barren desert, and he longed to have the same communion with the Lord in the desert as he had in the temple.

When rains do not come, we experience drought. If the trees could talk, they would probably cry out for water. The lack of water brings drought and the leaves turn brown unless they are in an area where they can get moisture. David experienced spiritual drought out in the wilderness. He referred to it as being a dry and desolate land without water. David was out in the desert away from the presence of the Lord. He could not go to the temple to worship. He longed for those days. There was a time in my life when it seemed I went through a spiritual drought. I felt like I had lost the sweet fellowship I had with the Lord. It was difficult to study my Bible and to pray. I felt like I was out in the wilderness all alone. One day I got down on my knees and I cried out to God admitting my neglect of spending time with Him daily and my desire to restore my fellowship with the Lord. I spent time on my knees just pouring out my heart to God and seeking His forgiveness. "I WAITED patiently for the LORD; and He inclined to me, and heard my cry" (Psalm 40:1, NASB). The Lord heard and answered my prayer. I arose from that place relieved of my spiritual drought.

The Master's Touch

My husband, Doyal, loves to restore old trucks. He is totally a Ford man and will not purchase a vehicle that is not made by Ford. He believes they are of the best quality and will last the longest. In the past, he has restored a 1946 Ford pickup that is very well done. He is now in the process of restoring a 1939 Ford two-ton flatbed truck. He enjoys working on flathead engines because this is the type of engine his father taught him how to rebuild as a boy. Our boys are amazed at how their Dad can envision in his mind exactly what he needs to do to rebuild something that has deteriorated. If he needs a particular tool he does not have, he builds the tool. God has truly given him an inventive mind. When the vehicle he is working on is completed, it looks like it has experienced the master's touch.

Nehemiah was in the city of Susa serving as the cupbearer for King Artaxerxes. Some men came from Judah. Nehemiah inquired about those who had been in captivity and also concerning the city of Jerusalem. He was informed that the wall around Jerusalem had been broken down and the gates had been burned by fire. When Nehemiah heard the news he sat down and mourned for days. He went before the Lord fasting and praying. Nehemiah was sad over the condition of Jerusalem.

> So the king said to me, "Why is your face sad though you are not sick? This is nothing but sadness of heart." Then I was very much afraid. And I said to the king, "Let the king live forever. Why should my face not be sad when the city, the place of my fathers' tombs, lies desolate and its gates have been consumed by fire?"
>
> Nehemiah 2:2-3 (NASB)

Nehemiah then requested that the king allow him to return to Judah so he could rebuild the wall around the city. He then asked the king for letters that he could give to the governors beyond their province so he could get the materials he would need. He wanted the very best of materials to use in the rebuilding of the wall.

When he arrived, Nehemiah inspected the wall at night. The next day he informed all the officials, the Jews, the priests, the nobles and those who would do the work what needed to be done. "Then I said to them, "You see the bad situation we are in, that Jerusalem is desolate and its gates burned by fire. Come, let us rebuild the wall of Jerusalem that we may no longer be a reproach" (Nehemiah 2:17, NASB). After Nehemiah told them how God had looked with favor on him and how the king had spoken to him, they were ready to begin rebuilding the wall. He told them that the God of heaven would give them success. They met with many obstacles during the building of the wall, but God led them all the way. "And it came about when all our enemies heard of it, and all the nations surrounding us saw it, they lost their confidence; for they recognized that this work had been accomplished with the help of our God" (Nehemiah 6:16, NASB). The wall around Jerusalem was now completed, the city was secure, and so the people worshiped the Lord. It was made with the very best of materials.

Doyal takes antique trucks and restores the body, engine, and all the other parts so they are like new. One would never know it was the same vehicle because it is a magnificent truck to behold. He had to replace the broken pieces to restore the truck to its original form. It truly displays the touch of a master craftsman.

Nehemiah's heart was broken when he heard about the condition of his home city. He prayed and sought God's guidance. God led him in all that he did and when the wall was finished, its appearance showed the touch of the Master's hand.

Doyal's truck is an example of the touch of a master craftsman. The wall around Jerusalem was evidence of the touch of the Master's hand. What about your life? Can others see the touch of the Master's hand on your life? If you do not know Jesus, you need the touch of the Master's hand on your life. Admit you are a sinner. Repent and ask the Lord to forgive you of your sin. Confess Him before others as your Savior and Lord. Pray, thanking Jesus for saving you. Your life should be a picture of the touch of the Master's hand.

The Steeping of Tea Leaves

Tea is a beverage made by pouring boiling water over dried tea leaves. Tea is considered to be the most popular beverage in most countries. When I was growing up my mother had a little tea strainer made out of aluminum. The bottom egg-shaped part had small holes all over it and there was a screw on lid with a small chain and it had a hook on the end of it. Mom would place the tea leaves in the strainer, no tea bags back then, and drop it in boiling water. She would hook the chain on the top edge of the pan and put the lid on the pan. She would let it boil for a short time and then take it off the burner and let the tea leaves steep. Mom would take the strainer out and then add the mixture to a pitcher of water. Some people like to drink tea without sugar and others like tea with a lot of sugar so it is very sweet to the taste.

When the tea leaves steep in the boiling water for long periods of time, the darker or stronger the tea will be. If steeped too long, it is almost bitter to the taste. If sin is allowed to remain and fester in our life, it will infect every part of our being. The darkness of sin controls our life because we have failed to confess it to God.

The children of Israel were instructed to march around the city of Jericho seven times. At the seventh time, the priests blew the trumpets and Joshua told the people to shout for the Lord had given them the city. When the walls fell, they burned the city and placed all the articles of silver, gold, bronze, and iron into the treasury of the Lord's house. They were not to take any of these items for themselves. But, Achan disobeyed and took some of these devoted things. The Lord's anger burned against them.

Some of the men were sent to Ai to spy out the land. The men returned and reported that there was no need for all of Israel to go against Ai because there were only a few men.

> So about three thousand men from the people went up there, but they fled from the men of Ai. And the men of Ai struck down about thirty-six of their men, and pursued them from the gate as far as Shebarim, and struck them down on the descent, so the hearts of the people melted and became as water.
>
> Joshua 7:4-5 (NASB)

The effects of sin can have a very demoralizing effect on the people.

Joshua and the elders fell down before the ark of the Lord with great mourning.

> So the LORD said to Joshua, "Rise up! Why is it that you have fallen on your face? "Israel has sinned, and they have also transgressed My covenant which I commanded them. And they have even taken some of the things under the ban and have both stolen and deceived.

> Moreover, they have also put them among their own things. Therefore the sons of Israel cannot stand before their enemies…"
>
> Joshua 7:10-12a (NASB)

All Israel was brought before Joshua by tribes and the Zerahites were taken. The families of this tribe then came before Joshua and Achan was found guilty. He had taken a beautiful Babylonian robe, two hundred shekels of silver, and a wedge of gold weighing fifty shekels. They took these items and all that belonged to him, his family, his animals, and his tent to the Valley of Achor. "And all Israel stoned them with stones; and they burned them with fire after they had stoned them with stones" (Joshua 7:25b, NASB). After the one who had sinned and all that belonged to him were destroyed, the Lord turned from His fierce anger against Israel.

What happens in your life when you have unconfessed sin? How does it keep you from being successful in what you are doing? Sin in our life separates us from God. There is no way we can have a close relationship with the Lord until we have confessed our sin. The sin in our heart begins to fester like a sore and it grows bigger and bigger. It hinders us from living a successful life for the Lord. When we sin, we must immediately confess our sin to the Lord and seek His forgiveness.

Satan Never Gives Up

The afternoon before we were leaving on a trip to teach people about Jesus, I was out in our flowerbed setting up a sprinkler to water the flowers. Our flowerbed is made out of old railroad ties and is two railroad ties high. Over the last thirty-one years the ties had warped and had begun to rot. At one end of the flowerbed the ties had warped in such a way that there was space for a person to step between the ties to get up in the bed. I had already stepped up in the flowerbed once and decided that I needed some iron stakes to stabilize the sprinkler, so I got down out of the flowerbed and went to get the stakes. Upon my return, I went to step in between the ties and just happened to look down. There was a large diamond-back rattlesnake lying in between the ties.

My husband was in the living room watching TV, so I immediately ran to the picture window and began pounding on it to get his attention. Finally, he came to the door and I told him about the snake. While he was putting on his boots and getting his .22 rifle, the snake slithered farther into the ties and only a part of his body was showing. Doyal shot him several times in the body, but he knew it would not kill him, so he told me go in the house and get some wasp spray. We sprayed it in between the ties where his head would be and slowly he began to slither backwards. Eventually, after another round of spray, he turned around and headed in the other direction. Doyal was then able to kill him by shooting him in the head. Think about how close I came to possibly being bitten by a poisonous snake. Satan seems to work up to the very last minute trying to deter us from going to serve the Lord. "If I walk in the thick of danger, You will preserve my life from the anger of my enemies. You will extend Your hand; Your right hand will save me" (Psalm 138:7, HCSB). After John baptized Jesus in the Jordan River, he witnessed the Spirit of God descending from heaven like a dove and settling on Jesus. "Then Jesus was led up by the Spirit into the wilderness to be tempted by the Devil" (Matthew 4:1, HCSB). Jesus had fasted forty days and forty nights, so He was hungry. Satan told Jesus that if He was truly the Son of God He could tell the stones to become bread. "But He answered, "It is written: Man must not live on bread alone but on every word that comes from the mouth of God" (Matthew 4:4, HCSB).

Satan led Jesus to the highest point of the temple and told Him to throw Himself down. If he were the Son of God, the angels would lift Him up. "Jesus told him, "It is also written: Do not test the Lord your God" (Matthew 4:7, HCSB).

The devil then led Jesus to a very high mountain and showed Him all the kingdoms of the world. He told Jesus he would give them to Him if He would bow down and worship him. "Then Jesus told him, "Go away, Satan! For it is written: Worship the Lord your God, and serve only Him" (Matthew 4:10, HCSB).

Satan then left Jesus for a time and the angels came and ministered to Jesus.

This scripture tells us that Jesus defeated Satan many times. Because of the victory over Satan by Jesus, we too are able to be victorious over the tempter. Jesus won many battles against Satan, culminating with His final victory on the cross. "When He had disarmed the rulers and authorities, He made a public display of them, having triumphed over them through Him" (Colossians 2:15, NASB). We must know the scripture and trust the Lord to help us when Satan comes against us. Where do you turn when Satan tempts you? The only place a Christian should turn is to the Lord for protection because He promises that He will not allow us to be tempted beyond what we can endure.

> No temptation has overtaken you but such as is common to man; and God is faithful, who will not allow you be tempted beyond what you are able, but with the temptation will provide the way of escape also, that you may be able to endure it.
>
> 1 Corinthians 10:13 (NASB)

We need to know scripture so we can rebuke the devil and tell him to leave us alone. When Jesus told Satan to get away from Him, Satan left him for a time. But, Satan will never give up.

Worry—Negatives Developed

Driving to McAlester, Oklahoma, one day, I saw this quote on a church sign: "Worry is the darkroom where negatives are developed." It caught my attention immediately. So many people worry about everything in life. Worry is like an infectious disease. The more we let it go without treatment the worse it gets. The dictionary defines worry as, "to feel or express great anxiety; a cause of anxiety." All of us at times have been guilty of worrying about something we can do nothing about, things that only God can change. "Don't worry about anything, but in everything, through prayer and petition with thanksgiving, let your requests be made known to God" (Philippians 4:6, HCSB). If we would pray and seek God's guidance rather than worrying, life would be so much easier.

In the late 1970s, our son, Anthony, sang in a children's musical at the church we attended in Riverside, California. The musical was about the fruit of the Spirit and his song was about patience. I don't think I will ever forget the words of that song. "Be patient, be patient, don't get in such a hurry. If you get impatient, you really start to worry." There is a lot of truth in the words of the song. When we get impatient with others or the situation we are in, we tend to get stressed out or worried about everything.

The story of Mary and Martha in the Bible is a familiar story. Mary and Martha had sent a message to Jesus that Lazarus was sick and close to death. But, Jesus did not go immediately. He stayed two days longer where He was before going to Bethany. Jesus knew exactly what He was going to do in order that the Father would be glorified. When He arrived in the city, Martha went out to meet Him. She told Jesus that if He had been there her brother would not have died. Mary told Jesus the same thing when she met Him. Mary sat at Jesus's feet listening to Him talk, but Martha was busy preparing the meal in the kitchen.

> But Martha was distracted with all her preparations; and she came up to Him, and said, "Lord do You not care that my sister has left me to do all the serving alone? Then tell her to help me." But the Lord answered and said to her, "Martha, Martha, you are worried and bothered about so many things; but only a few things are necessary..."
>
> Luke 10:40-42a (NASB)

Martha was worried about many different things and particularly that Mary was not helping her prepare the meal. Jesus said that Mary had chosen to listen to His teaching and that was something that could not be taken away from her.

Abram and Sarai left the land of Canaan and went to Egypt because there was famine in the land. Worry engulfed Abram's mind and heart as he came close to Egypt.

> When he was about to enter Egypt, he said to his wife Sarai, "Look, I know what a beautiful woman you are. When the Egyptians see you, they will say, 'This is his wife.' They will kill me but let you live. Please say you're my sister so it will go well for me because of you, and my life will be spared on your account.
>
> Genesis 12:11-13 (HCSB)

Because of worry and the scheme Abram contrived, he almost lost his wife and would have except for God's intervention. Worry causes one to make unhealthy decisions.

Instead of worry, you must "Trust in the LORD with all your heart, and do not rely on your own understanding; think about Him in all your ways, and He will guide you on the right paths" (Proverbs 3:5-6, HCSB). "Worry is the darkroom where negatives are developed." What do you do when life takes a sudden turn causing turmoil in your life? Do you trust in God and the strength only He can give or do you start to worry? Think about a time of turmoil in your life and write it in your journal. Possibly you immediately started to worry, but hopefully, you prayed to God and asked Him to help you bear your burden. Record in your journal how God helped you through this time of turmoil.

Friendship of Years Ago

God has a way of bringing very special people into our life. In June of 2009, the librarian from First Baptist Church in Heavener, Oklahoma, came to a book signing I had at a Christian bookstore in Poteau, Oklahoma. She purchased my recently published devotional book, Never the Same Again, for the church library. She knew the people of the church would be interested in the book because I was a 1962 graduate of Heavener High School. She put a note in the church bulletin that they had a new book in the library by Nancy (Farrell) Rowland. This caught the eye of my former high school Home Economics teacher. She checked the book out of the library so she could read it. She wrote me a very complimentary note after she read the book and told me she would love to visit with me. I did not recognize the name because it had been forty-eight years since I had graduated from high school and I had not seen her since that time. She gave me her phone numbers and since she was from Heavener, I decided to call her. She recognized my voice immediately, but I still did not know who she was. Realizing I was completely in the dark about her, I asked, "Am I supposed to know you?" She responded by telling me she was my high school Home Economics teacher. I immediately apologized for not recognizing her name. This was the beginning of a great friendship , but on a completely different level than we had as teacher and student. She has become a special friend in my life. We visit via phone and have a meal together every few weeks. True friendship is a gift from God that creates contentment in our life. "Oil and perfume rejoice the heart; so does the sweetness of a friend's counsel that comes from the heart" (Proverbs 27:9, AMP).

Jesus gave a good description of friendship as He was teaching His disciples. "You are my friends, if you do what I command you. No longer do I call you slaves, for the slave does not know what his master is doing; but I have called you friends, for all things that I have heard from My Father I have made known to you" (John 15:14-15, NASB). The Lord had a special relationship with the twelve apostles who traveled with Him from place to place. Jesus shared with these men what God the Father had said to Him. In the previous verses, He had explained to them how they must stay connected to the vine, which was Jesus, in order that they could live productive lives for Him. They must live their lives in obedience to Him doing as He commanded them to do. There would be times in their lives when the Father would have to prune away those things that hindered them from serving Him with all their heart. This was done in love and would help them as they sought to teach others about Him. They were special friends to Him and Jesus shared with them His very heart and soul.

A friend is one we can share our heart with and know that the things we share will stay with him or her and not be shared with others. "A friend loves at all times, and a brother is born for a difficult time" (Proverbs 17:17, HCSB).

If you know Jesus as Savior, you are considered to be God's friend as you live your life in obedience to Him. Are you consistent in cultivating your relationship with the Lord? Many times we allow other things to interfere with our personal relationship with the Lord. If something better comes up, we do not take part in the activities of His church. God expects our loyalty to Him because He is loyal to us. Do you think God would consider you to have an intimate friendship with Him? When you have a true, intimate friendship with someone you want to spend time with that person. If we have that type of relationship with the Lord, we will want to spend as much time as possible with Him. My former high school teacher has become one of my closest friends. I am always checking on her to see how she is doing and I enjoy doing things for her. I can share special things with her and know that they will not be told to anyone else. The Lord wants us to check in with Him throughout the day. I can truly say that my best friend is Jesus. What about you?

God's Purpose Accomplished

A peach is a round, edible fruit with the inside usually being yellow. It has a hard, deeply pitted stone in the middle. The flesh of a peach can be soft or quite firm. According to the encyclopedia, the peach tree was first planted in the state of Virginia around 1629 when the colonists settled there. It is amazing that a seed as hard as the pit of a peach can be planted in the late summer and after a time the seed cracks open and a sprout comes out of it. From this sprout comes a seedling; and my husband tells me that it must be dug up and replanted in a different place in order for it to grow. When it is replanted, young shoots called a bud are grafted onto the seedling. This is the way they get the many different varieties of peaches such as Glo-Haven, Bellaire, Loring, and many others. In the years to come the peach tree will grow fifteen to twenty-five feet tall. The pink flowers will come on the tree first and then the leaves. It will take about three or four years for the tree to produce a large crop of peaches. This is all a part of God's plan. "Then God said, 'Let the earth sprout vegetation, plants yielding seed, and fruit trees bearing fruit after their kind, with seed in them, on the earth;' and it was so" (Genesis 1:11, NASB). The Lord had a purpose for every tree that He created.

The peach tree requires sunshine and plenty of rain or water to produce beautiful peaches that are sweet to the taste. A healthy peach tree will produce fruit for around twenty years. If a peach tree is left to itself without care, it will not produce a large crop of good peaches. A peach tree must have the proper care and pruning in order to produce sweet, edible fruit.

Jesus left Judea and headed north towards Galilee. He did not go through Samaria by accident. An unusual encounter took place when Jesus stopped and visited with a Samaritan woman. It was strange because not only was she a woman, but she was a Samaritan and Jesus was a Jew. Jewish men did not normally talk to a woman particularly a Samaritan woman. It was by divine appointment because He would meet this woman at the well and offer to her living water. "Jesus answered, "If you knew the gift of God, and who is saying to you, 'Give Me a drink,' you would ask Him, and He would give you living water" (John 4:10, HCSB). She questioned Jesus as to how He was going to draw this water when He did not have a bucket.

> Jesus said, "Everyone who drinks from this water will get thirsty again. But whoever drinks from the water that I will give him will never get thirsty again—ever! In fact, the water I will give him will become a well of water springing up within him for eternal life.
>
> John 4:13-14 (HCSB)

Jesus had planted the seed and as He visited with her He questioned her about her life. She listened as Jesus talked about her five previous husbands and that the man she was living with at that time was not her husband. Jesus began pruning away the weight of her sin that so entangled her. Jesus brought her to the point of repentance of her sin and a desire to have the living water He offered. She went to her village and began bearing fruit through her witness about what Jesus had done for her. Many people came to know Jesus by her witness but even more came to believe as they came to listen to Jesus teach.

A peach tree will grow and produce fruit when it receives nourishment from the sunshine, rain, and good soil. An unsaved person will come to know Jesus when seeds about salvation through faith in Jesus Christ are planted in their heart. It is necessary for these seeds to be cultivated and watered in order that they will take root and a person will come to know Jesus as Savior. Through this process, God's purpose is accomplished for people to be saved. A new believer must be taught the Word of God in order for them to grow and begin to produce fruit for the Lord.

Armed by God for Battle

For several days now I have seen an armadillo in a clearing down by Lake Wayne Wallace in Robbers Cave State Park. He is in the same spot each time so apparently there are grubs, beetles, or some type of food that he likes. This little creature has armor-like skin. Armadillo comes from a Spanish word meaning "little armored one" referring to the bony plates that cover its back, head, legs, and tail. It is a strange looking little creature that looks like a prehistoric animal. This is the only living mammal that wears shells like this. The armadillo's shell is his best protection. The shell is made up of many small pieces of bony armor that are fitted closely together. These pieces are hard and stiff but they are jointed across its back. Because of this jointed armor, the armadillo can curl into a small ball and it is hard for other animals to get a grip on it with their teeth or claws. This small animal has a protective covering that other animals do not have.

The Philistines were camped between Sucoh and Zekah. The Israelites camped in the Valley of Elah. The Philistines had possession of many of the surrounding areas and now they wanted possession of the Valley of Elah. The Israelites lined up for battle. The Philistines were standing on one hill and the Israelites were on another hill with a valley between them.

> Then a champion named Goliath, from Gath, came out from the Philistine camp. He was nine feet, nine inches tall and wore a bronze helmet and bronze scale armor that weighed 125 pounds. There was bronze armor on his shins, and a bronze sword was slung between his shoulders. His spear shaft was like a weaver's beam, and the iron point of his spear weighed 15 pounds. In addition, a shield bearer was walking in front of him.
>
> 1 Samuel 17:4-7 (HCSB)

Goliath taunted the Israelites trying to persuade them to send one of their men out to fight against him. The Israelites were intimidated by the massive armor and the size of Goliath.

The three older brothers of David were in Saul's army. David had been chosen by Saul to be his armor bearer. David would go back and forth between serving Saul and shepherding the sheep of his father, Jesse. One day Jesse sent David to take some food to his brothers and check on how they were doing. When David arrived at the camp of Saul's army, he went to find his brothers and check on their welfare. As he neared the line of battle, he heard Goliath's voice as he spoke his usual words taunting the soldier's of Saul. "Then the Philistine said, "I defy the ranks of Israel today. Send me a man so we can fight each other!" When Saul and all Israel heard these words from the Philistine, they lost their courage and were terrified" (1 Samuel 17:10-11, HCSB). David questioned the soldiers as to who this man was that would defy the armies of the living God.

David went to Saul and told him that he would go out and fight against Goliath. Saul told him he could not go because he was just a youth. David told Saul that he had killed lions and bears to protect his sheep. David then made a very important statement. "Then David said, "The Lord who rescued me from the paw of the lion and the paw of the bear will rescue me from the hand of this Philistine." Saul said to David, "Go, and may the Lord be with you"" (1 Samuel 17:37, HCSB).

Saul tried to dress David in his own military armor, but they were too heavy for David to wear. David took his staff, his sling shot and five smooth stones as he went out to meet Goliath. The Bible says that Goliath despised him when he saw this youth coming towards him. "David said to the Philistine: "You come against me with a dagger, spear, and sword but I come against you in the name of the Lord of Hosts, the God of Israel's armies—you have defied Him. Today the Lord will hand you over to me" (1 Samuel 17:45-46a, HCSB). David was armed with a protective shield from God Almighty as he went out to meet Goliath. The Philistine came toward the battle line and David ran quickly to meet him.

> "David put his hand in the bag, took out a stone, slung it, and hit the Philistine on his forehead. The stone sank into his forehead, and he fell on his face to the ground. David defeated the Philistine with a sling and a stone. Even though David had no sword, he struck down the Philistine and killed him."
>
> 1 Samuel 17:49-50 (HCSB)

God created the armadillo with armor-like skin that would protect him from danger. He also made his shell in such a way that he can roll up in a ball for protection. Goliath had every piece of armor available and felt that he was invincible. The problem with his armor was that there was an opening in the helmet on his forehead. David came out to battle with the only weapons he was acquainted with; a staff, a sling and a pouch with five smooth stones. David knew that God was with him and that God would protect him. God enabled David to place that stone in just the right place with his sling shot to kill Goliath. When God is in charge, victory will come.

Each day when you get up to prepare for work whether at home or out in the business world, you must ready yourself for battle. How do you prepare for battle?

> Stand, therefore, with truth like a belt around your waist, righteousness like armor on your chest, and your feet sandaled with readiness for the gospel of peace. In every situation take the shield of faith, and with it you will be able to extinguish all the flaming arrows of the evil one. Take the helmet of salvation, and the sword of the Spirit, which is God's word. With every prayer and request, pray at all times in the Spirit...
>
> Ephesians 6:14-18a (HCSB)

When you clothe yourself for battle in the armor provided by God, you are ready for battle. Are you ready for battle when you begin your day? Clothe yourself in these pieces of armor before you ever get out of bed. The Armadillo was ready for battle because God created him that way. David was ready with simple tools because he went out in the name and power of God. Goliath came up short because there was an opening in his helmet where David put the deadly stone. Don't be caught short, clothe yourself in God's armor.

God's Refining Process

Many different metals must go through a refining process before they are of great value. Products such as sugar beets and sugar cane must go through a refining process to produce the sugar that we eat. God uses different situations in our life to refine us and make us useful to him. Refine means to free from impurities or waste matter. How does a silversmith know when the refining process is complete? The silver is heated to a liquid and he can see his reflection in the molten metal.

Sometimes we disobey the Lord and walk in the ways of the world. Because of our separation from God, we get to the point where we feel we are unworthy of God's love. We begin to think that life is of no value to us. If we seek the Lord, we will find Him during these times. God comes to us and assures us that He is with us in every situation that we face. He will not leave us nor will He forsake us.

> I have called you by name; you are Mine! When you pass through the waters, I will be with you; and through the rivers, they will not overflow you. When you walk through the fire, you will not be scorched, nor will the flame burn you. For I am the LORD your God…
>
> Isaiah 43:1b-3a (NASB)

Beginning in the first part of the book of Isaiah, we find that the children of Judah were on trial for their rebellious attitudes and disobedience. “Oh—sinful nation, people weighed down with iniquity, brood of evildoers, depraved children! They have abandoned the LORD; they have despised the Holy One of Israel; they have turned their backs on Him” (Isaiah 1:4, HCSB). God brought charges against them through Isaiah the prophet. God had made a contract with them in Deuteronomy 28 where God had specified that if they would be obedient to Him, they would be blessed. When they broke this contract with the Lord by outwardly disobeying Him, they brought punishment on themselves. They would be cursed rather than blessed. Later in the book of Isaiah the children of Israel continued to be a stubborn and obstinate people. They had closed their ears to the Lord. God promised He would not completely destroy His people, but a remnant would survive the judgment. “Look, I have refined you, but not as silver; I have tested you in the furnace of affliction” (Isaiah 48:10, HCSB). Subjecting silver to high temperature and removing the dross purifies it. God sought to refine Israel through the furnace of affliction. They were not worthy of God’s salvation, but because of His great love for them, He saved them from their affliction.

When we are disobedient to the Lord, He has ways of correcting us and taking us through the refining process. God must get rid of the impurities or waste matter in order that we can be used for His honor and glory. Silver and gold must go through a refining process before it is of great value. Sugar beets and sugar cane must be refined before we can have the pure sugar we eat and use in cooking. Can you think of a time in your life when you were living in rebellion against the Lord and in order to get your attention He took you through the refining process? How did you feel as you went through these times of refining or testing? How did you feel once you began to walk in obedience to the Lord?

Wisdom for All

Have you ever wondered why bears hibernate? This question came to my mind the other day so I decided to do some research about bears. When fall turns to winter and the temperatures drop, the food source for a bear becomes very scarce. Some animals wait out the harsh conditions of winter constantly searching for food, but the bear goes into hibernation. By the bear going into hibernation, he bypasses winter when his food supply of nuts and berries is not available.

In order for the bear to survive the harsh conditions of winter as he is cuddled up in a cave or hollow tree, he builds up his body weight by accumulating fat. The weeks before he goes into hibernation a bear will gain up to forty pounds of fat per week. The body of a bear goes through several changes during hibernation. His heartbeat will drop from fifty-five beats per minute to around ten beats per minute and the temperature of his body will drop five to nine degrees below normal. During his time of hibernation, he will use the accumulated fat he has stored to survive the winter. A bear can lose from fifteen to forty percent of its body weight during the winter by sleeping.

The book of Proverbs tells us that God gives wisdom even to the small creatures around us.

> Four things are small on the earth, but they are exceedingly wise: the ants are not a strong folk, but they prepare their food in the summer; the badgers are not mighty folk, yet they make their houses in the rocks; the locusts have no king, yet all of them go out in ranks; the lizard you may grasp with the hands, yet it is in kings' palaces.
>
> Proverbs 30:24-28 (NASB)

God also made the bear a wise creature by knowing that he must store up body fat to sustain him through the winter.

If God offers to all these creatures the wisdom to care for themselves, what does He offer to us? "The fear of the LORD is the beginning of wisdom, and the knowledge of the Holy One is understanding. For by Wisdom your days will be many, and years will be added to your life" (Proverbs 9:10-11, HCSB). What does the scripture mean by fear of the Lord? We are to come before Him with respect, reverence, or awe. We should come to worship God the Father with humility and respect, because He is a holy, righteous God.

The bear is wise in storing up body fat for the winter when food is not available. We gain wisdom by coming in reverential fear before the Lord seeking knowledge and understanding of Him. "God resists the proud, but gives grace to the humble" (James 4:6b, HCSB). What happens if you come to the Lord with the wrong attitude? First, you must confess your sin to the Lord. Not being respectful of the Lord is a sin. Second, you must pray asking God to forgive your bad attitude. Some people are too prideful to follow God's leading and they think they can do things their own way. They have no respect for the Lord and the life He desires for them. "The fear of the LORD is the beginning of knowledge; fools despise wisdom and instruction" (Proverbs 1:7, NASB). We serve a wise God who offers instruction to us. Seek wisdom from Him.

The Giant Redwood

When I was in college at California Baptist College in the 1960s, we went to an International Student Retreat in Northern California. On our way back home, we drove through the redwood forest. It was an amazing sight to behold. The massive trees within this forest were unbelievable. The tallest known tree in the world—368 feet—is in this forest. One of the trees that we saw was wide enough that they had cut a tunnel through it where any vehicle eight feet wide and under could drive through the middle of the tree. It proved to me that we should never underestimate the creative power of Almighty God. The same God that created these massive trees, also created all the hundreds of types of butterflies, birds, fish, animals, and plants we have today.

God created the different bodies of water that the Israelites encountered on their journey to the land of Canaan. The Lord had parted the Red Sea as the children of Israel headed toward the promised land and they walked across on dry ground. During the harvest season the Jordan River overflowed its banks, but as soon as the feet of the priests carrying the ark touched the water, the water began piling up at a place upstream. The children of Israel were able to walk across the Jordan on dry ground to enter the land of Canaan.

They entered near the city of Jericho, but the town was shut up tight. The people of Jericho had heard what God had done at the Jordan River for the Israelites and were paralyzed with fear. God gave Joshua specific instructions as to what they were to do.

> And the LORD said to Joshua, "See, I have given Jericho into your hand, with its king and the valiant warriors. And you shall march around the city, all the men of war circling the city once. You shall do so for six days. Also seven priests shall carry seven trumpets of rams' horns before the ark; then on the seventh day you shall march around the city seven times, and the priests shall blow the trumpets. And it shall be that when they make a long blast with the ram's horn, and when you hear the sound of the trumpet, all the people shall shout with a great shout; and the wall of the city will fall down flat, and the people will go up every man straight ahead.
>
> Joshua 6:2-5 (NASB)

When the Israelites did as they were instructed and they had marched around the city the seventh time, the priests blew the trumpets and Joshua told them to shout for the Lord had given them the city. They did as Joshua said and the wall fell down around the city.

Only God, the Creator of all things, could cause something like this to happen with the marching around the city, the blowing of the trumpets, and the shouting of the people. What things have happened in your life that you knew could not have happened without the divine intervention of the Lord? Think about your life and things that have happened because God intervened in your life. Make a list and then take time to pray and thank God for what He has done. Things do not happen by accident. God knows before it happens what is going to take place in your life. He uses all things that happen to teach you the principles of life. What are some of the life principles we learn through the experiences we have? We need to depend on the Lord in every situation. God is in control. When you have a need, call on Him. God is in all places at all times. God is concerned about every aspect of your life. God will give you the strength to be able to stand up against anything that happens. God loves you far beyond your imagination. Praise God in the good times and even in what you consider to be the bad times.

Lessons from a Hickory Nut Sprout

I was working out in our flower bed the other day trimming shrubs and putting wells around our shrubs so we could keep them watered more easily. As I was digging in the dirt, I found a hickory nut with the hull still partially around it and the shell of the nut split open. Out from between the two sections of the shell of the hickory nut was a sprout a little over an inch long. In a short time, the sprout would have started pushing its way up through the surface of the dirt. I know many times I have tried to pull a sprout out of the flower bed and it was almost impossible to do. Doyal told me that if you were able to pull one up, you would find the nut still attached to the sprout. This explains why they are difficult to pull up. What really got my attention was that the sprout was connected to the meat of the hickory nut.

It reminded me of the scripture:

> [Most] blessed is the man who believes in, trusts in, and relies on the Lord, and whose hope and confidence the Lord is. For he shall be like a tree planted by the waters that spreads out its roots by the river; and it shall not see and fear when heat comes, but its leaf shall be green. It shall not be anxious and full of care in

> the year of drought, nor shall it cease yielding fruit.
>
> Jeremiah 17:7-8 (AMP)

I don't know about you, but I can just see the roots of that tree spreading out towards the river and even reaching out into the riverbed in order to have the moisture it needs for its leaves to always be green and for it to continue to bear fruit. My husband tells me that when a time of drought comes, the roots of a tree will go down deeper and deeper in the earth searching for moisture in order for it to have the nourishment it needs. It could be compared to the sprout being connected to the meat of the nut. It does not stand there idle allowing the drought to destroy the life of the tree, but it seeks out nourishment from deeper places. The amazing thing is that through the process of searching for moisture, its root system becomes stronger and stronger.

When times of testing or trials come into our lives, how do we respond? Have we put down roots deep into the Word of God so that we are connected to the true meat of the Word? "Consider it a great joy, my brothers, whenever you experience various trials, knowing that the testing of your faith produces endurance. But endurance must do its complete work, so that you may be mature and complete, lacking nothing" (James 1:2-4, HCSB). James is telling us to turn these times of testing into times of learning. Through these times, we learn patience, perseverance, or steadfastness. All of us know that when we persevere through these times and stay faithful to the Lord that our roots go down deeper and deeper into His love.

> ...that Christ may dwell in your hearts through faith; that you being rooted and grounded in love, may be able to comprehend with all the saints what is the width and length and depth and height—to know the love of Christ which passes knowledge; that you may be filled with all the fullness of God.
>
> Ephesians 3:17-19 (NKJV)

As we endure these tough times, we realize just how great the love of our gracious and loving Father is for us. He gives us strength and power to persevere and at the same time to learn from Him and grow in Him

The sprout burrows its way up through the surface of the earth still connected to the meat of the hickory nut. In time, it will grow into a strong tree. If our relationship with the Lord is as it should be and we continually feast on the meat of his Word, applying it to our daily living, we will be able to stand strong like the hickory tree.

Be Still—
The Power of the Switch

All of us can remember hearing our parents say, "Be still." When I was growing up, churches did not have nurseries or children's church. Children sat beside their parents during the worship service. As my father was preaching, my mom expected me to sit quietly and listen to what was being said. I cannot remember, but I doubt that my mother carried books for me to read or pages for me to color. I was to sit up and listen. My mother carried the switch of persuasion in her purse. She would take a small branch off of a tree and place it in her purse. Any of you that have been disciplined with a switch know how much it stings when it is used to administer punishment for disobedience. The only thing my mother had to do was open her purse and let me see the switch for me to sit up and pay attention. "Train up a child in the way he should go, even when he is old he will not depart from it" (Proverbs 22:6, NASB). My parents took seriously the words of this verse.

God put Moses in charge of leading the Israelites out of slavery in Egypt to the promised land. God did not lead them through the land of the Philistines that was the shortest way, but He led them toward the Red Sea. The Lord went ahead of them with a pillar of cloud by day and a pillar of fire by night. The Lord told Moses that He would harden Pharaoh's heart and he would pursue them with his great army. As Pharaoh approached the Israelites, they began to question Moses as to why he led them out in the wilderness to die. They said it would have been better for them to die in Egypt serving the Egyptians than to die in the desert. "But Moses said to the people, "Do not fear! Stand by and see the salvation of the LORD which He will accomplish for you today; for the Egyptians whom you have seen today, you will never see them again forever. "The LORD will fight for you while you keep silent" (Exodus 14:13-14, NASB). The Israelites had no choice but to place their faith and trust in the Lord to do as He said He would do. More than likely there was much murmuring by some as they waited. Moses told them to sit quietly and wait upon the Lord to act. The scripture tells us that the Lord parted the Red Sea and the Israelites walked across on dry ground. When the Egyptians entered the walkway through the Red Sea, God caused major confusion and the waters covered them.

Our Father desires to have our attention at all times. “Be still, and know that I am God;” (Psalm 46:10a, NKJV). We need to have those times in our life when we come and sit quietly before the Lord and listen as He speaks to us through His Word, prayer, His people, events in our life, and things around us. There must be times when He wants to say to us, “Will you please stop squirming and be still so I can speak to you?” The Lord wants to refresh our mind and spirit and give us what is needed to face the things that happen in life.

“He makes me lie down in green pastures; He leads me beside quiet waters” (Psalm 23:2, NASB). According to one commentator, these quiet waters were inlets or ponds where one could find refreshment. We can imagine being beside a quiet stream where we might see our reflection in the clear waters. As we sit quietly before the Lord, we can praise God for all He has done in our life and thank Him for what He is going to do in the days ahead. In the quietness of this time, we seek His counsel and direction for our life. "I waited patiently and expectantly for the Lord; and He inclined to me and heard my cry" (Psalm 40:1, AMP).

Mother knew how to keep me quiet in church and the Lord certainly knows how to get my attention and cause me to sit quietly before Him. It was important for me to be quiet in church so others could listen to the message. It has been extremely important for me to learn how to sit quietly before the Lord and listen to His direction. I have found this so true in the writing of devotions. Personally, I will not hear Him speak to me if I am noisy. I need to be quiet and away from things that so easily distract me. One way we can quiet our spirit is to get on our knees before the Lord and pray to Him for guidance. Another way I have found that helps is to have quiet Christian instrumental music playing. For me, it is especially the old hymns of faith that quiet my spirit. We can go outside in the midst of God's creation and praise Him for all He has done. Sitting beside a pond or a stream of water is soothing and has a way of helping us listen to the Lord and what He has to say to us. Reading the Word of God is so important and unless we sit quietly as we read our Bible, we will not hear God speak to us.

A Light in the Midst of Darkness

The firefly is an amazing little creature. It is actually from the beetle family. There are about two thousand different species of fireflies. They have a lifespan of about two months and they are up to one inch in size. On a warm summer night you can see the lights flashing out in the pasture around our house. As a child, I loved to catch the fireflies, which we called lightning bugs, in a jar so I could watch them more closely. I would punch holes in the lid of the jar to give them air so they would stay alive. It was fascinating to watch them up close. As I did research about the lightning bugs, I found that in many places they use the fireflies for decoration and for light. Cuban women would sometimes pin a firefly called a "click beetle" on their gowns or attach one to a golden chain. People in tropical countries sometimes put many in a bottle and use them for lanterns. They give their light in flashes but when many are in a bottle, there is some flashing at all times giving light constantly. People who are traveling through deep tropical forests at night sometimes attach them to the toes of their boot to give light to the path in front of them.

Since the lifespan of the firefly is normally two months, they do not have long to mate and produce more fireflies. If we as believers had only two months to live, would it change the way we are living? The United States of America and the rest of the world are heavily populated with people who do not know Jesus Christ as Savior. If your lifespan was short, what would you do?

> For everyone who calls on the name of the Lord will be saved. But how can they call on Him in whom they have not believed? And how can they believe without hearing about Him? And how can they hear without a preacher? And how can they preach unless they are sent? As it is written: How welcome are the feet of those who announce the gospel of good things!
>
> Romans 10:13-15 (HCSB)

We are not here on this earth just to be a decoration as the firefly might be on a Cuban woman's gown or necklace. Jesus gave specific instructions to the disciples just before He ascended into heaven. "…but you shall receive power when the Holy Spirit has come upon you; and you shall be My witnesses both in Jerusalem, and in all Judea and Samaria, and even to the remotest part of the earth" (Acts 1:8, NASB). We are to be witnesses of His saving grace in Jerusalem, our home town. We are also to be witnesses in Judea, the state in which we live. We are to go to Samaria and this would be throughout every state in the United States of America. We are also to carry the good news of the gospel to people in the remotest parts of the earth.

Jesus stated very distinctly what He was to be to people. "Again therefore Jesus spoke to them, saying, 'I am the light of the world; he who follows Me shall not walk in the darkness, but shall have the light of life'" (John 8:12, NASB). When we accepted Jesus as Savior, we received the light. We would no longer walk in the darkness of sin. It is now our responsibility to be the light to a dark, sinful world. "You are the light of the world. A city set on a hill cannot be hidden. Let your light shine before men in such a way that they may see your good works, and glorify your Father who is in heaven" (Matthew 5:14, 16, NASB).

The firefly gives light wherever it is whether in a pasture, on a person's shoe in a tropical forest, or in a jar. Will you be a light to the people consumed by the darkness of sin by taking the good news of the saving grace of Jesus to all people? Anytime you share your testimony of how you were saved with someone, you are being a witness for the Lord.

God's Healthiest Plant

In the Spring of the year, people prepare their garden spots for planting. They plant all types of vegetables and fruits. In most of the gardens in our area tomatoes, cucumbers, squash, lettuce, radishes, corn, okra, and potatoes will be planted. We find that the first plants to come up will be different types of weeds. It seems that weeds thrive in a garden and become very large if they are not dug up. We wonder why God made the weeds when they seem to be such a nuisance.

My husband was telling me this morning that in the spring his grandmother would gather what they called lamb's quarters so that she could have some greens to eat. Since I am beginning to have an inquisitive mind as I search for things to write about, I went to the internet and typed in "weed—lambs quarters." It was amazing all the articles that were found. After seeing the plant, I realized I had seen it many times around our garden and corral. The writer of the article said that the leaves and stem are edible and delicious. The greens can be boiled or one can eat them raw in salads. Isn't it amazing how we consider so many things to be weeds and dig them up and throw them away?

Jesus taught many different teachings using parables. These are stories, especially those of Jesus, told to provide a vision of life, especially life in God's kingdom. In the book of Matthew, we have the parable of the wheat and the weeds.

> He presented another parable to them, saying, "The kingdom of heaven may be compared to a man who sowed good seed in his field. But while men were sleeping, his enemy came and sowed tares also among the wheat, and went away. But when the wheat sprang up and bore grain, then the tares became evident also. And the slaves of the landowner came and said to him, 'Sir did you not sow good seed in your field? How then does it have tares?' And he said to them, 'An enemy has done this!' And the slaves said to him, 'Do you want us, then, to go and gather them up?' But he said, 'No; lest while you are gathering up the tares, you may root up the wheat with them.' Allow both to grow together until the harvest; and in the time of the harvest I will say to the reapers, "First gather up the tares and bind them in bundles to burn them up; but gather the wheat into my barn."'
>
> Matthew 13:24-30 (NASB)

Satan is always at work trying to destroy those who believe. He does all he can to take the Word of God from their hearts, but when he cannot he tries other methods. If Satan cannot uproot those who are true Christians, he will sow counterfeit Christians in their midst. We have this happening in our world today where these counterfeit Christians are swaying people away from beliefs based on the Bible and into those beliefs built on false doctrine. We must be prepared as a believer when this happens and be able to stand against false teaching. "But sanctify the Lord God in your hearts, and always be ready to give a defense to everyone who asks you a reason for the hope that is in you, with meekness and fear;" (1 Peter 3:15, NKJV). We know that the hope that we have is because of Jesus coming to earth, being crucified, and shedding His blood on the cross in order that we might have forgiveness of sin. He was buried in the tomb, but the grave could not hold Jesus and on the third day He rose again that we might have the promise of everlasting life when we come to accept Jesus as Lord and Savior.

Weeds will grow into healthy plants wherever the seeds may fall. As believers, we must sow the Word of God and bear fruit in the place where God has planted us. On our jobs, in our homes or out in our community, as believers, we must be a living example for the Lord Jesus. Others must be able to see Jesus in us by our speech, our actions and in our business dealings. We are an extended arm of the Lord Jesus in a confused world. I was told as a child, "you may be the only Bible a person may read today" and I have strived to live my life in accordance with God's Word. It is difficult to tell the true from the false in these days, but when the end of the age comes, the angels will separate the true Christians from the false Christians. If the Lord were to come today would you be amongst the sheep, the true Christians, or would you be amongst the goats, the false Christians of this world? You must know where you stand and if you do not know Jesus, accept Him today. This is the most important decision you will ever make. You do not want to be a false Christian, but you want to be a true Christian that produces fruit for the Lord.

A Crafty Little Creature

We were going to be away from home for a couple of weeks so we asked some friends to keep check on our house and dog while we were away. Our dog, Daisy, was accustomed to eating her food from a dog feeder on the back porch so she did not require much care. A raccoon found the food and apparently was coming each night to eat from the dog feeder. Our friends watching over our home and dog said that one day they found the dog feeder in the yard and they thought it was the work of a raccoon. When we returned, one morning I flipped on the light on the back porch, opened the door, and sure enough there was a big, fat raccoon. We moved the feeder to the front porch and for a few weeks we only put out enough food for our dog to have each day . We then began putting more food in the feeder, because the raccoon had not yet found it. In March of 2011, we heard the dog barking loudly and sure enough the raccoon had found the feeder once again. At night, we have to put a concrete block in front of the feeder door to keep the raccoon out of the food. They are crafty and intelligent creatures.

The Israelites went into battle against the people of Ai. It amazes me how God in His wisdom and planning told Joshua exactly what to do in order to defeat Ai.

> Now the LORD said to Joshua: "Do not be afraid, nor be dismayed; take all the people of war with you, and arise, go up to Ai. See, I have given into your hand the king of Ai, his people his city, and his land. "And you shall do to Ai and his king as you did to Jericho and its king. Only its spoil and its cattle you shall take as booty for yourselves. Lay an ambush for the city behind it."
>
> Joshua 8:1-2 (NKJV)

Joshua did exactly what God told him to do. All the men of Ai saw the Israelites across the valley and went out to attack them. After the men left the city, another group went in and burned it to the ground. They did not realize there was a group waiting to ambush them from behind. When Joshua and his group saw that the city was burning, they turned and came from the other direction. The entire population of Ai was destroyed that day. Joshua consulted God and did as God said.

In Joshua 9, we read of the guile, deception, or craftiness of the Gibeonites. The Hittites, Amorites, Canaanites, Perizzites, Hivites, and Jebusites had combined their armies to fight against the army of Joshua and the Israelites. But, the Gibeonites had their own plan of how to survive.

> But when the inhabitants of Gibeon heard what Joshua had done to Jericho and Ai, they worked craftily, and went and pretended to be ambassadors. And they took old sacks on their donkeys, old wineskins torn and mended, old and patched sandals on their feet, and old gar-

> ments on themselves; and all the bread of their provision was dry and moldy.
>
> Joshua 9:3-5 (NKJV)

They told Joshua and the men of Israel that they had come from a distant land to ask them to make peace with them. Joshua and the Israelites questioned from where they had come and sought to know more about them.

The Gibeonites said they had heard of all their great God had done in Egypt and how they had defeated the two Amorite kings east of the Jordan. They came declaring their people to be their servants and to ask for peace. They showed them how their bread was molded, clothing and sandals worn, and their wineskins were old and cracked. "Then the men of Israel took some of their provisions; but they did not ask counsel of the LORD" (Joshua 9:14, NKJV). They signed a peace treaty with them and three days later they found out the truth. They found they had been deceived by the Gibeonites. They could not kill them, but they made them their servants.

The raccoon was such a crafty little creature and it mattered not where we put the feeder, he seemed to find it. Finally, the raccoon and our dog got into a scuffle and we have not seen him for quite some time. We must be alert to the antics of Satan. Being wise and seeking God's counsel is necessary in the life of a believer. God will give us directions to do what He desires if we will seek His counsel. Satan is crafty and will deceive us.

Brewed to Perfection

Coffee is considered to be the favorite drink in almost every country particularly those in temperate or cold climates. Coffee beans grow on a tree, but it is sometimes referred to as a shrub. At maturity, it may be fourteen to twenty feet tall. The coffee tree is usually five years old before it bears a full crop of beans. The average tree bears enough beans each year to make about one and one-half pounds of roasted coffee. It is quite a process to get the beans ready to roast. After being separated by an extensive process, the beans are ready to roast in a roaster oven. When they are roasted, they are stored in bins to later be ground into drip, regular or fine grain coffee.

People around the world enjoy coffee brewed at different strengths. Some people like weak coffee, some medium strength coffee, and many like coffee brewed so strong it is almost bitter to the taste. When we went to Brazil, we learned very quickly not to order coffee in a restaurant. They serve it to you in a very tiny cup and it is extremely strong. It is so black that you cannot see the bottom of the cup.

The different strengths of coffee, weak, medium, and strong, can be compared to the spiritual strength of born again believers today. We have many very weak Christians that have not really matured in the Lord.

Paul in his letter to the Corinthians said that he could not talk to them as mature Christians. He had to talk to them as if they still belonged to the world or as though they were still infant Christians. "I gave you milk to drink, not solid food; for you were not yet able to receive it. Indeed, even now you are not yet able, for you are still fleshly" (1 Corinthians 3:2-3a, NASB). Some people have no desire to grow in the Lord; they simply want to bear the name Christian.

Our churches are full of medium Christians. They are somewhere between the weak and the strong. They dabble in the things of the Lord. The medium Christian will read the Bible from time to time, but they do not spend time searching the scriptures and meditating on the Word of God, so they can mature as born again believers.

> How can a young man keep his way pure? By keeping it according to Thy word. With all my heart I have sought Thee; do not let me wander from Thy commandments. Thy word I have treasured in my heart, that I may not sin against Thee. I will meditate on Thy precepts, and regard Thy ways.
>
> Psalm 119:9-11, 15 (NASB)

The Word of God gives instruction as to how a believer can grow in Him. The prayer of our heart should be that these medium Christians will spend time in the scriptures.

The last type of believers are those who are strong. One who desires to grow in the Lord will have a hunger and thirst for the Lord and His Word. "O GOD, Thou art my God; I shall seek Thee earnestly; my soul thirsts for Thee, my flesh yearns for Thee..." (Psalm 63:1a, NASB). David expressed it well as he was out in the dry desert and he had a desire to be in the presence of the Lord. "As a deer pants for the water brooks, so my soul pants for Thee, O God" (Psalm 42:1-2a, NASB).

A strong Christian will strive to develop a true love relationship with the Lord and to grow in their understanding of His Word. Are you weak, medium, or strong for the Lord? In order to grow in the Lord, you must be a part of a growing church fellowship. Be sure you go to a Bible believing and Bible teaching church. As you sit under the teaching of the Word of God, you will become stronger in your faith. Spend time doing Bible studies by Christian authors that will give you discipline in studying God's Word. After you have done this for awhile, you will be able to open the Bible and do study on your own. Always mark the things you want to remember and make notes in a journal or notebook. Writing things down helps us to remember what we have studied. Work at growing in the Lord. It will be the most incredible journey of your life. Your coffee may be weak, medium, or strong, but may your walk with the Lord be strong.

God's Unusual Provider

The raven is a very large bird that averages two feet tall. It can have a wingspan as large as fifty-six inches. They are at times confused with their cousins the crow, but a raven weighs up to four times as much as the crow. It is written that they are excellent acrobatic fliers on par with the falcons and hawks. They are known as scavengers, but they are also excellent hunters. Teams of ravens have been known to hunt game too large for a single bird. They help themselves to the eggs of many different birds and also feast on rodents, grains, worms, and insects. Ravens often dine on carrion and human garbage. According to the dictionary, carrion is dead and decaying flesh.

God used this very unusual prospect to provide food for the prophet Elijah. Why would God use a bird like a raven that is a scavenger and many times partakes of dead and decaying flesh? The raven was considered an unclean bird and was detestable in the eyes of the people. It was on the Mosaic list of forbidden foods. Yet God used this bird to sustain the life of this prophet.

The Jewish people were dependent on the rains that God sent for the success of their crops. If God did not send the rains in October and November and later in March and April, they would soon have a famine in the land. Whether or not God sent the rain depended on the people obeying the covenant of the Lord.

> And it shall come about, if you listen obediently to my commandments which I am commanding you today, to love the Lord your God and to serve Him with all your heart and all your soul, that He will give the rain for your land in its season, the early and late rain, that you may gather in your grain and your new wine and oil. And He will give grass in your fields for your cattle, and you shall eat and be satisfied.
>
> Deuteronomy 11:13-15 (NASB)

If they did not obey the Lord and they turned away to serve other gods, the anger of the Lord would be shown against them. He would shut up the heavens and there would be no rain. The ground would not yield the fruit of the harvest that they needed to live.

King Ahab did more to provoke the Lord than any other king. He had led the people to serve Baal and worship him. God sent Elijah the Tishbite with a message for Ahab. "As the Lord, the God of Israel lives, before whom I stand, surely there shall be neither dew nor rain these years, except by my word" (1 Kings 17:1b, NASB). God had a special plan for Elijah. "Go away from here and turn eastward, and hide yourself by the brook Cherith, which is east of the Jordan. And it shall be that you shall drink of the brook and I have commanded the ravens to provide for you there" (1 Kings 17:3-4, NASB). God used this scavenger bird that many times feasted on dead and decaying flesh to provide food for Elijah. We would not think about using something that was considered to be unclean to provide food for a human. But, our God moves in mysterious ways far beyond our comprehension. Elijah survived because of God's provision of water from the brook and the ravens coming with food for him to eat in the morning and the evening. What an amazing God we serve that makes provision for us in every situation in life if we simply will ask.

Right now in our area, we are in the midst of a drought. We are in dire need of rain. Do you think God might be withholding rain from us because of our disobedience to His commands? Born again believers need to pray and seek God's guidance in their lives daily.

The Act of Forgiveness

My husband and I have just returned from a few days of vacation in Branson, Missouri. We love going to Branson in November or December because the different entertainers do Christmas shows and much of Branson is decorated for Christmas. Silver Dollar City is decorated with millions of lights. It is a sight to behold. While we were there, we went to see a theatrical adaptation of Charles Dickens's A Christmas Carol. Ebenezer Scrooge is the main character in the story. He was quite wealthy and treated those who worked for him or borrowed money from him with contempt. He was very demanding of his employee Bob Cratchit. He hardly paid him enough wages for him and his family to survive. When Christmas came, Mr. Scrooge demanded that the debts be paid. It seemed he had no compassion for others and certainly not a forgiving spirit. He hated Christmas time. The ghost of Christmas Past took him on a journey back to his own childhood. He was also made to see the conditions of the Cratchit family with Tiny Tim being crippled and the parents having no money to help him. Through it all, Ebenezer Scrooge's attitude about Christmas was changed. He became a loving, compassionate man.

In the book of Matthew, we find a story about forgiveness. Peter approached Jesus concerning how many times we should forgive others. Peter suggested that possibly he should forgive those who sin against him seven times. "Jesus said to him, 'I do not say to you, up to seven times, but up to seventy times seven'" (Matthew 18:22, NASB). In the scripture, there was a king who wanted to settle the debts owed to him by his slaves. There was a man who owed him ten thousand talents and according to the Amplified Bible this was ten million dollars. The man could not pay and the king demanded that he be sold along with his wife and children and all they possessed so the debt could be paid. "The slave therefore falling down, prostrated himself before him, saying, 'Have patience with me, and I will repay you everything.' And the lord of that slave felt compassion and released him and forgave him the debt" (Matthew 18:26-27, NASB). This slave had been shown compassion and had his debt forgiven.

The slave did not practice the same compassionate spirit that his owner had shown to him. Instead, he went out and found a slave that owed him money and when he could not pay, he had him thrown into prison until he could pay back what he owed. When his lord found out about it, he ordered his slave to be brought to him. "Should you not also have had mercy on your fellow slave, even as I had mercy on you?" (Matthew 18:33, NASB). His lord had him handed over to the torturers until he could repay his debt. The heart of this particular scripture has a message for each of us, "So shall my heavenly Father also do to you, if each of you does not forgive his brother from your heart" (Matthew 18:35, NASB).

When Ebenezer Scrooge revisited his past and then was made to see how he was responding to others in the present, his heart was changed. He showed a compassionate, forgiving spirit toward others. It is an example to us of how we are to be forgiving of others. People must be able to see Jesus in us. Some people may never pick up a Bible and read it, but when they see Jesus in us, they may be drawn to Him. They may come to accept Jesus as Savior because of our example. God forgave us of our sin and we must show the same forgiveness to those around us.

Are you willing to forgive others when they do wrong against you? Are you guilty of saying you forgive someone, but you still have an unforgiving heart toward that person? Jesus set the example for us on the cross as to how we are to forgive others. One of the statements spoken by Jesus while He was hanging on the cross set the example for us. "But Jesus was saying, "Father, forgive them; for they do not know what they are doing" (Luke 23:34a, NASB). He had a forgiving spirit even while suffering the agony of the cross. The thief hanging on one of the crosses beside Jesus spoke to Jesus. "And he was saying "Jesus, remember me when you come in Your Kingdom!" And He said to him, "Truly I say to you, today you shall be with Me in Paradise"" (Luke 23:42-43, NASB). In spite of the suffering Jesus was going through, He had compassion on the man hanging beside Him and forgave him of his sin. We must always have a forgiving spirit in every circumstance in our lives if we are going to follow Jesus's example.

Desire to Flee

The other night I went fishing in our pond. I was not getting any strikes so I decided to move to a different section of the pond. I cast my lure out around the lily pads. All of a sudden, a fish grabbed the hook. I knew it was a bass because the fight was on as I tried to bring it to shore. It would dart back and forth from one batch of lily pads to another. I was afraid it would get tangled up around the lily pads, but I continued reeling it in as it tried to flee from me. I finally got it to shore. It was only about eight or nine inches long, but it was determined to try to get away from me while in the water and out of the water.

Have you ever had a time in your life that you have betrayed a friend by repeating something they did not want you to share with anyone? Maybe, you have failed to stand up for the Lord and be a witness for him because you were afraid others would ridicule you. Did you feel guilty after you failed to do what was right? Judas Iscariot betrayed Jesus for thirty pieces of silver. Jesus knew when they were eating the last supper together that Judas was the one that would betray Him. During the dinner He told the disciples that one of them would betray Him.

> And being deeply grieved, they each one began to say to Him, "Surely not I, Lord?" And He answered and said, "He who dipped his hand with me in the bowl is the one who will betray me. The Son of Man is to go, just as it is written of Him; but woe to that man by whom the Son of Man is betrayed! It would have been good for that man if he had not been born."
>
> Matthew 26:22-24 (NASB)

Even Judas Iscariot questioned the Lord saying that surely it was not him. Later in the garden of Gethsemane, Judas Iscariot identified Jesus. "And immediately he went to Jesus and said, 'Hail, Rabbi!' and kissed Him" (Matthew 26:49, NASB). Because of fear, all of the disciples fled from the garden when they arrested Jesus.

The next morning after the chief priests and the elders reconvened to confirm the arrest of Jesus; they bound Him and led Him away to Pilate.

> Then when Judas, who had betrayed Him, saw that he had been condemned, he felt remorse and returned the thirty pieces of silver to the chief priest and elders, saying, "I have sinned by betraying innocent blood." But they said, "What is that to us? See to that yourself."
>
> Matthew 27:3-4 (NASB)

We know from the scripture that Judas went away and hanged himself. Some believe that the remorse that Judas showed was not one of repentance that led to sorrow for his sin, but his remorse was regret that he had been caught. This led him to despair and then to suicide.

There was no way in the world that Judas could get away from the sin he had committed and neither can we. It matters not where we go, until we come before the Lord in complete repentance for the sin we have done, it will follow us wherever we go. Judas's sin was very evident and there was no way he could deny it. He admitted he had betrayed innocent blood, but he did not repent. The Lord gave us specific instruction as to what we are to do when we sin. "If we confess our sins, He is faithful and righteous to forgive us our sins and to cleanse us from all unrighteousness" (1 John 1:9, NASB). The bass tried every trick it could find to keep me from reeling it into shore. It was determined to flee from me as it sought refuge in the lily pads. Being alert to the antics of the fish was important if I was going to get the fish to shore.

Satan loves for us to try to flee from the presence of the Lord. My prayer for all of us today is that we will not live our lives running from the sin we have committed, but that we will repent and seek God's forgiveness. "He who has my commandments and keeps them, he it is who loves Me; and he who loves Me shall be loved by My Father, and I will love him, and will disclose Myself to Him" (John 14:21, NASB). Live your life in obedience to the Lord and experience His great love for you.

The Trials of Life

Often, we fail to think about the trials people have gone through to get to where they are today. I think of my parents who spent most of their years in the ministry working in small churches. My mother shared with me the problems they had years ago when my dad was pastor at Elm Grove Baptist Church. The church paid my dad forty dollars a month because that was all they could afford. This was the only income they had to live on, so they had to be extremely careful what they did. My dad would set traps for rabbits and they would have rabbit dumplings, rabbit stew, and fried rabbit. They planted a garden, and when their garden and those of others in the church were ready to harvest the women would get together to can the food. They would share with Mom and Dad some of the produce from their garden to help supplement their salary.

When they were at this church, my parents had my two oldest sisters. It was a struggle to make ends meet, but knowing my mother, I am sure she did not complain. When she was sharing with me about this experience, she had a joyous spirit about the time they spent with the people of that church. Trials are not always negative, because God blesses through those times. "Consider it all joy, my brethren, when you encounter various trials, knowing that the testing of your faith produces endurance" (James 1:2-3, NASB). Many times in their ministry, my parents encountered difficult trials, but they praised God for what He was doing and how He was using them to His glory.

The movie The Nativity seems to be a good portrayal of the struggles Mary and Joseph went through. Her parents betrothed Mary, as a young woman, to Joseph. The betrothal lasted for one year before they ever lived together as husband and wife. During this time, Mary was found to be with child by the Holy Spirit. "And Joseph her husband, being a righteous man, and not wanting to disgrace her, desired to put her away secretly" (Matthew 1:19, NASB). Joseph assumed that Mary had been unfaithful to him by having relations with another man. Certainly, this must have caused Mary even more confusion as she was trying to deal with the fact that the Holy Spirit had impregnated her. Knowing how we are, humanly speaking, she was probably criticized by others who were aware of her situation. The Lord appeared to Joseph in a dream and told him not to be afraid to take Mary as his wife, because the baby in her was conceived by the Holy Spirit. Can't you imagine how difficult the trials must have been as they dealt with this miraculous happening? Even though they encountered difficulties, they experienced great joy when Jesus was born.

Trials come to all of us, but how we handle these difficult times shows the depth of our relationship with the Lord. "Blessed is a man who endures trials, because when he passes the test he will receive the crown of life that God has promised to those who love Him"

(James 1:12, HCSB). A person who endures his trials is blessed. The word blessed according to the Holman Christian Standard Bible reflects a person who walks in the paths set by the Lord and sees his trials in terms of the hope that awaits him when Jesus comes again. When we look at our trials from this perspective, they do not seem to be as bad. We can see God at work even in the midst of trials.

Many times it was a struggle for my parents when Daddy pastored small churches, but they always had fond memories of those times. They had no regret for the time spent with the good people of these country churches. God always provided for their needs in some way. Think about what you would do in situations such as these. It is beneficial to keep a journal of times in your life when things have really been tough, but in the midst of a stressful time, God has intervened and met your needs. It will help you be grateful that you serve a loving and gracious God. When the road gets tough and you feel you cannot continue on, look up; the Lord is waiting for you to ask for strength to endure these trials.

Frozen Stiff

When I was growing up, we did not have a clothes dryer until late in my teenage years. Almost everyone had a clothesline in the backyard. By that time, Mom did have an automatic washer and she would wash the clothes, put them in a basket, and send us outside to hang the clothes on the line. The funny thing about hanging clothes on the line in the winter months is that they would freeze stiff. It was rather entertaining to see all the different formations when a shirt, a pair of trousers, or a skirt would freeze. We could really let our imagination run wild. The simple things of life entertained us in those days before all the technological things were invented. Even though the clothes would freeze on the line from the cold temperatures when the sun came out the clothes would thaw and smell fresh and clean.

Many of our churches are cold and indifferent to the needs of our world today. We live in a completely different environment than we did when I was growing up. But, somehow some of our churches have failed to see the need of change in order to reach the newer generations of people. The message should not change because the Bible never changes. It is the same today as it was in the past and as it will be in the future. "For God loved the world in this way: He gave His One and Only Son, so that everyone who believes in Him will not perish but have eternal life" (John 3:16, HCSB). God loves all people. He sent His son to die upon the cross for the sin of people from all walks of life whether they are people living in mansions, out on a farm, or living under a bridge in a cardboard house.

His message is for all people and it matters not what country they are from. God's love far surpasses any cultural or societal barriers we may throw up. Sometimes Christian people are offended by those who have tattoos all over their bodies, by those who are dressed in black clothing with chains hanging from the waist or from pockets, or they may have their face, ears, lips, or nose pierced in many different places. Whether we are dressed in the finest of clothes or whether we are dressed in shabby clothes, the message of our Lord does not change. "For all have sinned and fall short of the glory of God" (Romans 3:23, HCSB). People everywhere need to know Jesus as Savior. The Lord does not distinguish between rich and poor, people who live on a beautiful ranch or on the streets of New York, nor whether we are dressed in the finest of clothing we can buy or if we have chains dangling from every part of our clothing. "But God proves His own love for us in that while we were still sinners Christ died for us" (Romans 5:8, HCSB)! Oh, how great our Father's love is for us that He would allow His only Son to die on the cross for our sin. There is no greater love found than the love of God for us. It is the same message for all people "If you confess with your mouth, "Jesus is Lord," and believe in your heart that God raised Him from the dead, you will be saved" (Romans 10:9, HCSB). We must believe that Jesus is the Son of God that He died on the cross for our sin, was buried, and God raised Jesus from the grave in order that we might have everlasting life. He makes a promise in His word that will not be broken. "For everyone who calls on the name of the Lord will be saved" (Romans 10:13, HCSB). When we come to Jesus confessing our sin and seeking forgiveness of our sin, we will be saved. He is always listening when we cry out to Him.

The warmth of God's love needs to thaw out the ice that has formed in many of our congregations and we need to accept people as they are. God looks at the heart not the way they look on the outside and we must do the same. We must not allow a hard freeze to cover the warmth of God's love for all people from every walk of life and from every nation in our world.

Destruction in Progress

It is amazing how certain things capture our attention as we go through life. When I was in high school in Heavener, Oklahoma, I was amazed at what would happen to the back window of our Home Economics Building each spring. The wooden frame of that back window would be covered with termites. They were amazing to watch, but they were very destructive to the wood around the window and the window sill. Thousands of termites worked diligently to destroy the wood.

We have been amazed in our travels to other countries to see termite mounds fifteen to twenty feet high. Our first impression was that the dirt in those mounds was no good, but as we talked with people we found that it is excellent material for making bricks. It seems there is a silicone in this dirt that helps to make a stronger brick.

When I think about how swarms of termites can completely destroy the wooden frame around a window, it reminds me of how we can become so entangled in sin that it completely destroys our life. Jeroboam had become king over the people of Israel. He led the people to worship idols.

> "If this people go up to offer sacrifices in the house of the LORD in Jerusalem, then the heart

> of this people will return to their lord, even to Rehoboam king of Judah; and they will kill me and return to Rehoboam king of Judah." So the king consulted, and made two golden calves, and he said to them, "It is too much for you to go up to Jerusalem; behold your gods, O Israel, that brought you up from the land of Egypt."
>
> 1 Kings 12:27-28 (NASB)

Not only did the king sin in doing this, but he led the children of Israel to sin by worshipping idols rather than God who had led them for many years. Jeroboam placed one of the golden calves in Bethel and one in Dan. "Now this thing became a sin, for the people went to worship before the one as far as Dan" (1 Kings 12:30, NASB). Jeroboam also built shrines on high places and appointed priests from among the people who were not Levites.

Jeroboam was standing by the altar in Bethel when God sent a prophet to him to prophesy what was going to happen. He prophesied that the altar would be split apart and the ashes on it would be poured out.

> So it came to pass when King Jeroboam heard the saying of the man of God, who cried out against the altar in Bethel, that he stretched out his hand from the altar, saying, "Arrest him!" Then his hand, which he stretched out toward him, withered, so that he could not pull it back to himself. The altar also was split apart, and the ashes poured out from the altar, according to the sign which the man of God had given by the word of the Lord.
>
> 1 Kings 13:4-5 (NKJV)

Other things happened concerning the prophet, but still Jeroboam did not turn from his evil ways. Eventually, his sin led to the downfall and destruction of the house of Jeroboam.

In other countries, the dirt in the huge termite mounds is used to make strong bricks. But, in our country, termites are destruction in progress as they eat away at and demolish the wood of a home or building.

Think about your life. Is there any sin that is eating away at your heart and mind today? Write that sin down in your journal, get down on your knees, confess it to God and seek His forgiveness. Jot it down in your journal the day you sought God's forgiveness. Don't allow sin to continue being destruction in progress as it eats away the joy of your salvation.

Follow the Leader

The other day as I was driving to a book signing, I noticed a herd of cattle walking on a beaten trail one behind the other. I asked my husband if the same cow would be the leader each time. He told me that in some herds there is a dominant cow that will always be out in front, but in other herds it might be a different leader each time. Even though the leader may be different, they will still follow their leader by walking in a line one behind the other.

I thought about a mama duck and her ducklings and how the mama is always out in front and the little ducklings are walking behind her in a straight line. They follow their mother whether walking or swimming.

When we were children, we played the game follow the leader. We would watch the leader and do exactly what that person did. If the leader skipped forward, we would all skip forward. When the leader changed his action, everyone would follow the leader.

Children follow the example set for them by their parents or an adult they admire. They want to be just like that person. When our children are growing up, we see them standing in the same way that we stand and using the same gestures and speech patterns that we use. Watching our children, we see a picture of ourselves. They are simply following their leader.

Jesus selected His twelve men to work closely with Him. "And Jesus said to them, 'Follow me, and I will make you become fishers of men'" (Mark 1:17, NASB). He had a specific reason for selecting the men that He did. He saw their potential and knew exactly how He would use them. As they traveled around the countryside, Jesus was continually teaching them things they needed to know. He demonstrated to them how to show compassion to others. He showed them how to respond when they were ridiculed and treated harshly by people. He told them what would happen to Him in the future and also to them.

He was a living example of what He wanted them to be. They were to imitate Jesus in the things that they did. "And He called the twelve together, and gave them power and authority over all the demons, and to heal diseases. And He sent them out to proclaim the kingdom of God, and to perform healing" (Luke 9:1-2, NASB). Jesus had been casting demons out of people and healing them of all types of diseases. By observing the example set by Jesus, the disciples were learning how to do the things Jesus intended for them to do when He called them to follow Him. According to the book of Mark, He sent them out in pairs. He gave them the authority to perform acts of healing and to preach the gospel or the Good News about Jesus. They were to follow the example that Jesus, their leader and teacher had set for them.

The cattle, ducks and other animals learn to follow the leader. Children and adults also adapt to following the leader. Are you learning to follow Jesus in a way that is pleasing to Him? Some people say they will follow Jesus, but it seems it was not a true commitment and they are not pleasing to God. The Lord always fulfills His promises to us and we should keep our promises to Him. Do not let other things come between you and your commitment to the Lord. If we make God our first priority, other things will fall in place. For instance, my husband and I both believe that if we make God our first priority, our marriage will be as it should be. We will be committed to God and committed to one another. But, we must work at keeping out marriage healthy and strong. God ordained marriage and we strive to follow His suggestions in how a marriage should be. When people look at your life and the things that you do, are they seeing a person imitating the Lord Jesus? We should be the same person at home, at work, at church or wherever we are. If we have the love relationship with Jesus that a Christian is supposed to have, it will be seen in the way we treat other people. We will show the love of Jesus to them and be willing to go the extra mile to help them. Jesus set the example for us as He went out of His way many times to help others. Even though He was tired, He was always ready to stop and minister to others. We should always be ready to assist others in any way we can.

Amazing Fruit

The apple is an amazing fruit. There are over 2500 varieties of apples in the United States and over 7500 varieties around the world. People have a variety of choices in apples, whether they want sweet apples to eat or tart apples to make a pie. Even in ancient Rome, apple trees were grown that produced prize fruit. According to the encyclopedia, it is thought that the Romans took apples with them to England when they conquered the country. The seeds of apples and apple trees were brought to America from Europe around 1628.

When I was teaching school, I would show the movie, The Legend of Johnny Appleseed, to my class each year. Johnny Appleseed was a real live person. He was actually John Chapman who was born in Massachusetts in 1774. This man was a US pioneer and a folk hero. He was trained as a nurseryman around 1800 and began collecting apple seeds from cider presses in Pennsylvania. He spent the next half century planting and tending apple orchards as far west as Indiana, usually ahead of settlers moving to that area. He felt the settlers needed fruit along with the wild game and fish found in the forests and streams. He traveled west to the Ohio River valley, planting seeds all along the way. He had over 1200 orchards of his own that he cared for along with hundreds of square miles of other orchards he tended. He would return once a year to tend to the orchards he had planted. He would sell the seedlings from the orchards, give them away, or sometimes trade the seedlings for whatever the people had. He went about doing good deeds for others.

In the Bible, we have the parable of the sower. As the sower went out to sow his seeds, some fell beside the road and people trampled on it and the birds came and ate the seed. Other seed fell on rocky soil and even though they took root, they did not last long because they did not have the water they needed. There was other seed that fell among the thorns but as the thorny plants grew they choked out the new plants coming up. Some of the seed fell on fertile soil and the plants flourished and produced one hundred times as much as had been planted.

Jesus went on to explain the meaning of this story.

> Now the parable is this: The seed is the word of God. Those by the wayside are the ones who hear; then the devil comes and takes away the word out of their hearts, lest they should believe and be saved. But the ones on the rock are those who, when they hear, receive the word with joy; and these have no root, who believe for a while and in time of temptation fall away. Now the ones that fell among thorns are those who, when they have heard, go out and are choked with cares, riches, and pleasures of life, and bring no fruit to maturity. But the ones that fell on the good ground are those who, having heard the word with a noble and good heart, keep it and bear fruit with patience.
>
> Luke 8:11-15 (NKJV)

When you read about the planting of the seed, where do you fit in? Have you heard the Word of God, but you have refused to follow Jesus? Maybe you are one, who heard about the Lord and received His message, but it was a superficial belief and your roots did not go down deep. Gradually, you fell away from the Lord because it was not a decision of the heart. Perhaps you believed, but the things of this old world were too enticing and you could not let go of what you thought brought joy into your life. But, maybe your heart was open to the Lord and the soil of your heart was fertile. When the seeds were planted and began to sprout, the teachings of God's Word took root in your heart. You have progressively matured in the Lord and in your service to Him. Johnny Appleseed planted apple trees so people could have fruit to make them healthy. How about you? What kind of seed are you planting in the hearts of people?

This Old House

All of us have seen what happens to a house when people no longer live in it. Before long, vandals begin breaking out the windows of the house. The shutters around the windows may lose a screw or two and when strong winds come they flop in the wind. The paint begins peeling off the outside of the house because no one is caring for it and keeping it presentable to the eye. The grass and weeds begin growing up around the house making it look desolate. The interior of the house begins to deteriorate because there is no heat or cooling. The paint begins peeling off the walls and the sheetrock becomes yellow. The tape and bedding may begin peeling off the sheetrock. The plumbing may freeze and burst in very cold weather because of the lack of heat. When the iron pipes are not used, they begin to collect rust deposits in them. Dust begins to collect in the corners of the house and cobwebs collect around the ceiling. Mice and rats may begin to inhabit the house. People who are vagrants may stay in the house on their way through town and they leave their trash when they move on. Without the loving care of the people who own the house, it begins to deteriorate. No one works at keeping it presentable.

As a believer, the scripture tells us exactly what our body is to be. "Don't you know that you are God's sanctuary and that the Spirit of God lives in you? If anyone ruins God's sanctuary, God will ruin him; for God's sanctuary is holy, and that is what you are" (1 Corinthians 3:16-17, HCSB). When we accepted Jesus as Savior, the Holy Spirit came to live in our heart. Wherever we go or whatever we do, the Holy Spirit is there with us. He is there to empower us, to strengthen us. He is within our hearts to remind us that we are the Lord's and we are to walk in the ways of the Lord. We should dress in a way pleasing to God because our body is the temple of God. We are to keep ourselves clean and pure without and within. We are to be living examples of Jesus Christ. "He who believes in me, as the Scripture said, 'From his innermost being shall flow rivers of living water'" (John 7:38, NASB).

I love the verses that speak about how we can keep ourselves pleasing to God.

> Beloved, if our heart does not condemn us, we have confidence before God; and whatever we ask we receive from Him, because we keep His commandments and do the things that are pleasing in His sight. And this is His commandment, that we believe in the name of His Son Jesus Christ, and love one another, just as He commanded us. And the one who keeps His commandments abides in Him, and He in him. And we know by this that He abides in us, by the Spirit whom he has given to us.
>
> 1 John 3:21-24 (NASB)

For most people, it is a continual work in progress to keep our heart, soul, mind and body dressed in the clothing of the Lord in order that we are presentable to Him. The Holy Spirit lives within our heart to guide us in living a life pleasing to God.

We must work to keep our relationship with the Lord strong so it will not deteriorate. If we allow it to deteriorate, not only will our heart and mind not be pleasing to the Lord, but our outward appearance will be a picture of what is taking place in our innermost being. We must take care of our body because it is the temple of God. We do not want our body to get in disarray as the house that was left empty without anyone caring for it. Radiate the love of Jesus to others this week because you have a living, vibrant relationship with the Lord. Be sure to keep His temple, your body, presentable to others.

Lessons Learned from a Dandelion

When I was a child, I loved to cut off a dandelion and blow on it so all the little feathery seeds would fly everywhere. The dandelion blossoms open in the morning and close in the evening. The blossom of a dandelion is a golden yellow head that is really a cluster of flowers. When the flowers ripen, they form feathered, cottony seeds that the wind carries far and wide. This is when we would love to blow them all over the yard not realizing that we were really planting seeds for more weeds in our yard. They are very hard to mow with a lawnmower. They will just bounce right back up after you mow over them. We either need to dig up the dandelion by the roots or we need to poison the weed in order for it not to continue growing.

Think about this illustration in relation to sin in our life. If we know we have sinned and we do not confess that sin to the Lord, it will begin to spread like a disease and affect every aspect of our life. Our countenance begins to change. Sin has become our first priority rather than the Lord. "Watch out, brothers, so that there won't be in any of you an evil, unbelieving heart that departs from the living God. But encourage each other daily, while it is still called today, so that none of you is hardened by sin's deception" (Hebrews 3:12-

13, HCSB). Hopefully, there will be those believers who will come along side us to encourage us to return to the Lord.

We have known people who appear to be walking closely with the Lord and all of a sudden they stop coming to church. They are no longer interested in things of the Lord. Bible study and times of prayer in their life cease. Associations or friendships with Christian people are broken off. Their life begins to fall apart. Even on their job, they do not perform as they had previously. Sin has a hold on their mind and their heart. Is their life completely without hope? No, it is not "For whatever is born of God overcomes the world. And this is the victory that has overcome the world—our faith. Who is he who overcomes the world, but he who believes that Jesus is the Son of God" (1 John 5:4-5, NKJV)? We must pray for these people and continue to encourage them to come back to the Lord. We serve a gracious and forgiving God who gives us victory when we feel it is beyond our reach. "Then I acknowledged my sin to You and did not conceal my iniquity. I said, "I will confess my transgressions to the LORD," and You took away the guilt of my sin" (Psalm 32:5, HCSB). David realized the need of confessing his sin to the Lord in order that he could be relieved of the burden of his sin and guilt. Confession of sin is a necessity in our lives today. We are assured in the Word of God that if we come to Jesus confessing our sin, He will forgive us of our sin.

The feathered, cottony seeds of a dandelion when blown by the wind all over the yard produce more weeds in our grass. Poisoning them or digging them up by the roots is the only way they can be destroyed.

Sin left to spread and grow as a disease in our life can only be removed by confessing our sin to the Lord. The scripture tells us that He will forgive us of our sin and restore us to a living, vibrant relationship with the Lord. This type of relationship is found only by abiding with the Lord through Bible study and prayer. We must seek to find a church, a fellowship of believers, who will encourage us in our walk with the Lord. Be certain that the church you attend preaches and teaches the truth of God's Word.

How Does Your Garden Grow?

During the first few years Doyal and I were married, we planted a garden out back of our house. Doyal prepared the garden spot by breaking up the ground with a plow. We then tilled the ground with a tiller to break up the clods. We planted the pieces of seed potatoes about twelve inches apart. The plants had just pushed their way up through the soil when an extremely hard frost came late in the season along with very cold weather. The plants just disappeared. I dug down into the soil where we had planted the potatoes and found nothing. We thought that our potato crop was lost. We decided to plant green beans in that area so Doyal put up two posts and strung several strands of wire between the posts. We planted Kentucky Wonder green beans that were climbing plants. As the runners from the bean plants grew, they just naturally attached themselves to the wire. We had a great crop of beans. All of a sudden, we noticed small plants coming up under the beans, so we dug down in the ground and there was a beautiful crop of white rose potatoes. We dug up enough potatoes to fill a paper towel box half full. They were delicious potatoes. God blessed us with green beans and potatoes all together in one spot. God certainly proved that all things were possible with Him.

In the Book of Genesis, we find that the first garden was planted. We have the beginning of man having to toil long, hard hours to grow a garden in order to have food. Adam listened to Eve and ate from the tree of the knowledge of good and evil in the middle of the garden. He chose to do this rather than doing what God commanded, so he was put out of the Garden of Eden and made to work the soil.

> The ground is cursed because of you. You will eat from it by means of painful labor all the days of your life. It will produce thorns and thistles for you, and you will eat the plants of the field. You will eat bread by the sweat of your brow until you return to the ground, since you were taken from it. For you are dust, and you will return to dust.
>
> Genesis 3:17b-19 (HCSB)

Prior to their sin in the garden, they were able to pick their food from a tree. Because of their sin, they would have to bend over to gather food from the plants of the field. Their work would be much harder physically. Adam would be required to do backbreaking labor planting seeds to grow vegetables to eat.

Seeds must be planted in order to grow a garden. Think of your life as a garden that is being planted. Will what is growing and flourishing in your life be for the good of others? What are the fruits of your labor? We should be growing the fruit of the Spirit. "But the fruit of the Spirit is love, joy, peace, patience, kindness, goodness, faith, gentleness, self-control. Against such things there is no law" (Galatians 5:22-23, HCSB). In order to grow this fruit, we must allow God to work the soil of our hearts and prepare them for planting. When our hearts are ready, we will produce fruit that will flow from within us to encourage others in their walk with the Lord.

When we planted a garden, we thought the hard frost had killed our potatoes so we planted green beans. God did an amazing thing by giving us potatoes and green beans. What we received was worth the effort we put forth to plant a garden. God made Adam and Eve leave their easy life in the Garden of Eden because of the sin they had committed. They had to labor long hours tilling the ground in order to plant a garden. Think about what we would have missed if the first garden had not been planted. We would miss all of those delicious fresh vegetables that people grow.

The Good Old Days in the Country

Years ago life was sure a lot simpler than it is today. When Doyal and I married, he told stories about picking cotton and how life was when he was growing up. My mom began telling stories about her life and how she would go to the cotton fields to hoe the weeds from around the plants. When the cotton was ready, they would pick the cotton. Life was not easy, but it was not hurried like it is today.

When we would go to see Mama Cordie, my mom's mother, she would go out in the yard, catch one of her fryers, ring its neck, dip it in hot water, and then pluck all the feathers out. They would then gut it and wash it good before cutting it up like a chicken is supposed to be cut with two legs, two wings, two thighs, a pulley bone, a breast, two side breasts, and the back. Nowadays they split a chicken down the middle and make huge pieces. They would also fry the gizzard, the liver, and the neck. My grandmother on my dad's side would even fry the head. Mama Cordie would then cook potatoes that they had grown in the garden along with other vegetables. She would make mashed potatoes with delicious chicken gravy. Almost everything came from what they grew in their garden.

Women would sit around shelling peas or snapping green beans and visit with one another. The men would sit out under a shade tree sharing all kinds of stories. They took time to visit with their neighbors. Riding horseback was the fastest way to travel a long distance. The wagon was a slower way to travel, but much needed for families. When my life gets so busy, I long for the good old days.

When a person comes to know Jesus as Savior, the Bible tells us what happens to their old way of life. "Therefore if any man is in Christ, he is a new creature; the old things passed away; behold, new things have come" (2 Corinthians 5:17, NASB). Christ died on the cross, shedding His blood to pay the price for our sin. When the Holy Spirit convicts our heart of the sin in our life, we must confess our sin and seek God's forgiveness. We must die to self and decide to live for Jesus. We have been born again, not of flesh, but of the Spirit. The process of transforming us into the likeness of Christ begins when there is a definite change in the life of the new believer. "And He was saying to them all, 'If anyone wishes to come after Me, let him deny himself, and take up his cross daily, and follow Me'" (Luke 9:23, NASB). Our outlook on life changes and we determine in our heart to live for Jesus rather than for self.

When life becomes so busy that it seems we do not have the time to rest and enjoy life, I think about how great it would be to live the slow pace of the good old days. In many ways, I would like to experience the joys people had of being together and sharing with one another. The good old days in the country were simple but joyous as people took time to visit with one another. But, when it comes to my life in Christ, I would not want to go back to the old days when I was walking in sin and had no relationship with the Lord. Knowing Jesus as Savior, I can continually converse with Him throughout the day and night. As I spend time with the Lord in the scripture, our friendship grows as I get to know Him better.

My prayer for you is that you can say, "My best friend is Jesus." He so wants to have an intimate love relationship with you. Won't you invite Him to sit and visit with you each day? He is just waiting for your invitation.

An Active Chemical Compound

Baking soda is used in many different ways. It is a chemical compound that is a fine powder. According to an article I read, it releases bubbles of carbon dioxide when it interacts with an acid and a liquid. The most common use for baking soda is as a leavening agent in cooking. Baking soda will make muffins soft and fluffy.

Baking soda is used for many different things. It can be added to your bath water to soften your skin. Taking a baking soda bath will relieve skin irritations. It can be used to relieve skin itch from insect bites and pain from sunburn. Baking soda mixed with water can be used as a mouthwash to relieve canker sore pain. A paste of water and baking soda can be applied to relieve bee or wasp stings. The list could go on and on with ways to use baking soda. One site I found listed seventy-five uses of the chemical compound of baking soda.

When baking powder is not available, baking soda can be used as a substitute, but the amount needed may be different. I was always thankful when we lived overseas to have baking soda available because baking powder was difficult to find.

If we eat very spicy foods or we eat too much at one time, we may have indigestion or heartburn. We can make a mixture of baking soda and water and use it as an antacid. We drink it to relieve the pain and misery caused by what we have eaten.

What happens in our life if we over indulge on the Word of God? "Thy words were found and I ate them, and Thy words became for me a joy and the delight of my heart; for I have been called by Thy name, O Lord God of hosts" (Jeremiah 15:16, NASB). Being filled with the Word of God brings joy and delight to our heart and soul, not heartburn that is caused by us eating too much rich or spicy food. "And He said to me, 'Son of man, feed your stomach, and fill your body with this scroll which I am giving you.' Then I ate it, and it was sweet as honey in my mouth" (Ezekiel 3:3, NASB). When Ezekiel filled his body with the words God gave to him, it was sweet as honey to his taste. He did not need the mixture of baking soda and water to settle his stomach from what he had eaten.

The psalmist said it well in his writings:

> O how I love Thy law! It is my meditation all the day. Thy commandments make me wiser than my enemies, for they are ever mine. I have more insight than all my teachers, for Thy testimonies are my meditation. How sweet are Thy words to my taste! Yes, sweeter than honey to my mouth!
>
> Psalm 119:97-99, 103 (NASB)

Overeating on the Word of God does not give us indigestion or heartburn, but it puts a taste in our mouth that is sweeter than honey. It makes us wiser than our enemies and gives us greater understanding of the scripture as we meditate on it day and night.

The Bible sets before us the most exquisite meal that we will ever be offered and we can eat as much as we want and not have heartburn. The Word of God will continually feed our heart and soul and it will cause us to want to dig deeper and deeper so we can satisfy our hunger with what God has to offer us. My prayer for you is that you will spend more time with the Lord in His word and it will be sweeter than honey to your taste. Don't worry about buying extra baking soda to help with your indigestion caused by overeating, because you will not need it when you overeat at the extravagant meal God sets before you.

The Cleansing Process of Friction

It seems they are not sure when the washboard was invented. Different dates as far back as the 1700s have been discussed. Some were made of grooved wood used to scrub clothes on. The washboards I have seen have a wooden frame and grooved metal on which to scrub the clothes. When we rub the clothes on the grooved metal, it causes friction that helps to cleanse the cloth of dirt and stains. As I was growing up, they referred to them as rub boards, because you were rubbing one thing against another.

While living in Malawi, we had some of the women wash our clothes when we were not where we had a clothes washer. When we were living in a cottage on the shores of Lake Malawi, the women would take our clothes down to the shore of the lake and use a bar soap they could buy in the village market to wash our clothes. We could hear them beating the clothes against a big rock to try to get the stains and dirt out of the cloth. Once again, there was the use of friction, the clothes beaten and rubbed against the rock, to try to get them clean. With this type of washing, we noticed that the nap of the cloth was removed by the continual beating against the rock.

Sometimes friction between two people can be used for good. In the book of Acts, we have the first missionary journey that Paul and Barnabas made to the island of Cyprus. John Mark accompanied them as their helper. When they left for Pamphylia, John Mark left them and returned to Jerusalem.

After some time, Paul felt it necessary for them to return to the places where they had proclaimed the word of the Lord to see how the people were doing. "And Barnabas was desirous of taking John, called Mark, along with them also. But Paul kept insisting that they should not take him along who had deserted them in Pamphylia and had not gone with them to the work" (Acts 15:37-38, NASB). It seems that Barnabas, whose name means son of encouragement, had a forgiving heart and even though John Mark had left them, he wanted to give him another opportunity to serve. Paul, on the other hand, was not as forgiving and more outspoken and did not feel they should take him because of him deserting them before.

> And there arose such a sharp disagreement that they separated from one another, and Barnabas took Mark with him and sailed away to Cyprus. But Paul chose Silas and departed, being committed by the brethren to the grace of the Lord. And he was traveling through Syria and Cilicia, strengthening the churches.
>
> Acts 15:39-41 (NASB)

Because of their disagreement or the friction between them as to who should go, two missionary journeys were made instead of one. More people heard the gospel and they were able to encourage more people in the cities where they had ministered before. Typically, friction is not good between members of a body of believers, but in this situation, God used it for good.

David asked the Lord to examine his heart. "Examine me, O LORD, and try me; test my mind and my heart" (Psalm 26:2, NASB). This should be the constant prayer of each child of God. It is good to know why we respond as we do. God uses this examination to cleanse our heart and mind. Sometimes the friction caused by rubbing one thing against another is very uncomfortable, but it is necessary for cleansing.

Washing of clothes by hand or with a washboard requires that a certain amount of pressure be applied causing friction in order to get the clothes clean. We should use the Word of God to cleanse our heart and mind when there is friction between believers.

Continual Mixing Together

One day I was driving behind a cement truck that was taking cement to a construction job andthe drum of the truck was turning round and round. Since Doyal is a concrete contractor, I identify with things such as this. Before this truck leaves the plant, they put a mixture of cement, sand, and rock into the drum along with a certain amount of water. They must continually keep this drum rotating in order to keep the materials mixing while in transport. There is a spiral blade on the inside of the drum that continually rotates in order that the mixture of the different materials will mix correctly and it will not begin to set up in the drum. When the blade rotates in one direction, it pushes the cement deeper into the drum. If the drum is rotating in the opposite direction, it will push the cement out and through a chute that enables it to be poured out inside of forms to make a floor, beams, septic tanks, and many different items. Now, think with me what would happen if there was not continual turning of the drum during transport or if the truck takes too long to get to the job. Doyal does not like for the truck to have to travel over an hour particularly in hot weather. The mixture gets too hot and begins to set up. If the cement sets up in the drum of the truck, they will need to take a jackhammer inside the drum to remove the cement.

What happens in the life of a born again believer if they do not stay active in the work of the Lord? We fail to mix with other believers who give us spiritual support. We allow ourselves to get so busy and entangled in other things that we begin to neglect our relationship with the Lord. Our heart begins to harden towards the Lord Jesus and we do not feel we need a close, intimate fellowship with Him. When we go to the house of the Lord to worship with fellow believers, there is a process of rejuvenation that takes place in our heart and life. Through the teaching and preaching of the Word of God, we are encouraged to grow in the Lord and to be active in sharing the gospel with others.

The scripture tells us point blank to not forsake the assembling of ourselves together.

> Let us hold fast the confession of our hope without wavering, for He who promised is faithful; and let us consider how to stimulate one another to love and good deeds, not forsaking our own assembling together, as is the habit of some, but encouraging one another; and all the more, as you see the day drawing near.
>
> Hebrews 10:23-25 (NASB)

There is something about being with God's people that revitalizes our spirit. When we listen to the preaching of an anointed man of God who believes and preaches the Word of God, it helps us to want a more intimate, vibrant relationship with the Lord. The Lord Jesus is not concerned about us doing more for Him, He wants us to have a more intimate relationship with Him that grows each time we study and meditate on scripture.

The people in the early church in the book of Acts set a good example for us. "And they were continually devoting themselves to the apostles' teaching and to fellowship, to the breaking of bread and to prayer" (Acts 2:42, NASB). It is difficult for a believer to grow spiritually if they neglect meeting together in the house of the Lord with fellow believers. I love the following verse from the book of Ephesians. "May Christ through your faith [actually] dwell (settle down, abide, make His permanent home) in your hearts! May you be rooted deep in love and founded securely on love..." (Ephesians 3:17, AMP).

The drum of a cement truck must be continually turning in order to keep the cement, sand, rock and water mixing together. The cement mixture will become hard if the drum is not continually turning. As a believer, it is important not to neglect meeting with fellow believers because it renews our spirit. If we do not spend time with fellow believers, our heart may become hardened concerning things of the Lord. Joining together with other believers in worship is needed for a person to grow in the Lord. After hearing the preaching of God's Word, our cup is filled to overflowing. It enables us to be a witness to others because we are revitalized from the continual mixing together with others who know Jesus.

The Story of the Honeybee

Did you ever wonder why honeybees make honey? I did some research on the subject and honeybees use the honey to provide energy for their flight muscles and for heating the hive during the winter months. They collect nectar from flowers and store it as honey in their hives. Honeybees also collect pollen that supplies protein for the bee brood to grow.

Honeybees live in colonies that are maintained, fed, and transported by beekeepers. After many centuries of selective breeding, they have produced a honeybee that produces far more honey than the colony needs. Many beekeepers harvest the honey and sell it. We had a gentleman in our church that raised honeybees as a hobby and he was always giving honey with the honeycomb in it for people to eat. It was delicious on hot biscuits, oozing with butter.

Not only do the bees produce delicious honey, but they also produce beeswax that is used for different things. The worker bees of a certain age will secrete beeswax from a series of glands on their abdomen. They use the wax to form the walls and caps of the comb. When the honey is harvested, the wax can be gathered to be used in various wax products like candles and seals.

Bees and honey are mentioned several times in the Bible. Samson saw a woman in Timnah that he decided he had to have as his wife. His parents questioned him as to whether there was not a woman amongst their own people that he could take as a wife rather than going to the uncircumcised Philistines for a wife. But, Samson was determined to have the woman from Timnah as his wife. "However, his father and mother did not know that it was of the LORD, for He was seeking an occasion against the Philistines. Now at that time the Philistines were ruling over Israel" (Judges 14:4, NASB). His parents did not understand that God was at work in this pursuit.

As they were traveling toward Timnah, a young lion came roaring towards Samson. "And the Spirit of the LORD came upon him mightily, so that he tore him as one tears a kid though he had nothing in his hand; but he did not tell his father or mother what he had done" (Judges 14:6, NASB). God gave Samson the strength to kill the lion. He proceeded on to Timnah and did not tell his parents what had happened. He saw the young lady and talked with her and he desired to have her as his wife. "When he returned later to take her, he turned aside to look at the carcass of the lion; and behold, a swarm of bees and honey were in the body of the lion" (Judges 14:8, NASB). When Samson looked at the carcass of the lion he had killed, he scraped some honey from the carcass and ate it. According to the Nazarite vow, which Samson had taken, he was to avoid touching any dead bodies. He then gave some of the honey to his mother and father, but he did not tell them it was out of the carcass of the lion. Bees produce honey in many different places.

God's Word is said to be sweeter than honey to the taste. "How sweet are Thy words to my taste! Yes, sweeter than honey to my mouth" (Psalm 119:103, NASB). Honeybees produce honey that is eaten all over the world and it is sometimes used to sweeten drinks or cookies. The beeswax from the honeycomb is used to make many different things. The honeybee is an important little creature in our world today.

How important do you think it is in your walk with the Lord for you to continually taste of the sweetness of God's Word? For me, it is extremely important to have a special time of study with the Lord daily. When I do this, I come away from that time knowing that I have been in the presence of the Lord. I have a sweet taste in my mouth as God has shown me things that will help me live for Him from His Word. When you spend time with God daily in His Word, how does it affect your relationship with other people and your relationship with Jesus Christ? The Word of God is an instruction book or a book of guidelines for our daily living. It helps us know how to relate to one another. The following passage is an example of what God expects from us. "Beloved, let us love one another, for love is from God; and everyone who loves is born of God and knows God. The one who does not love does not know God, for God is love" (1 John 4:7-8, NASB).

Changing Times

The other night I sat down in my easy chair for a few minutes before going to bed to relax and have a cup of hot tea. Doyal was asleep in his chair and the TV was on a channel with a show about all types of game hunts from turkey to water buffalo. The amazing thing to me was all of the different types of guns, bows, and computerized equipment they carried with them. They had the latest in guns with sights that would magnify what was in the brush. With the computers, they could tell right where the game was and actually see it through the brush. The bows they had were unbelievable. Not only were they extremely powerful, but also they had every type of razor head a person would need. They each carried a powerful rifle, a compound bow, and different types of computerized equipment. What happened to the day when a man went out to hunt with just a bow and a few arrows or with one rifle like a 30-30? Of course, they would not be of much use I guess in killing a huge water buffalo. There continues to be all kinds of changes to hunting equipment. The old is never quite good enough. I was thinking about that this morning as I was driving through the park from town and noticed some deer along the road.

Thanksgiving emerged from within my soul that the Word of God never changes. It is the same as it was years ago and today it is the same as it will be in the future. It will never change because God spoke the Word and the Holy Spirit inspired men to write it down. God's Word has been tested down through the ages. "Every word of God is tried and purified; He is a shield to those who trust and take refuge in Him" (Proverbs 30:5, AMP). Think about how the Word of God has stood through the years and has been the most popular selling book. It is a plumb line for our life. It is an instruction book concerning how we are to live our life. It is full of all types of literature. It is a book of mystery, a book of war and bloodshed, a book of miracles throughout the Old and New Testament, a book of love, and a book of occurrences that would be unbelievable if we did not know about the power of Almighty God.

Whoever heard of a donkey talking or an axe head floating to the surface from the bottom of a stream in this day and time? Who in this day and time has strength greater than Samson just because his hair has never been cut? Who could make a fig tree without fruit wither up, never to grow fruit again? The list could go on and on of unusual things in the Bible that only God could cause to happen. The Bible is really the greatest piece of literature ever written because it has every type of literature imaginable within its sixty-six books. "As for God, His way is perfect! The word of the Lord is tested and tried; He is a shield to all those who take refuge and put their trust in Him" (Psalm 18:30, AMP). It gives us strength for each and every day. He is a shield around us as we face the things of this world and we can find refuge under the shadow of His wing. "How precious is Your steadfast love, O God! The children of men take refuge and put their trust under the shadow of Your wings" (Psalm 36:7, AMP).

We don't need all the new fang-dangled equipment like the big game hunters do to hunt. We can discover the riches of God's Word by simply picking it up to read. God will reveal new things to us free of charge if we will spend time abiding in Him.

Seeking Protective Covering

My husband is a concrete contractor. One of the products he makes is a two piece storm shelter that can be installed in one day. There is a strong adhesive waterstop that goes between the top and bottom pieces of the cellar so it will not leak. The cellar will seat around eight people. This past storm season we had a long list of people wanting storm shelters because we had so many tornadoes. People seek a protective covering when a storm is coming. If they have a storm shelter to go to, they feel much safer.

When storms come in the life of a believer, where do they go for help and protection?

> The eyes of the LORD are toward the righteous, and His ears are open to their cry. The righteous cry and the LORD hears, and delivers them out of all their troubles. The LORD is near to the brokenhearted, and saves those who are crushed in spirit.
>
> Psalm 34:15, 17-18 (NASB)

The Lord is always listening for our cry, our call to Him, and He will rescue us in times of distress. "HE who dwells in the shelter of the Most High will abide in the shadow of the Almighty. I will say to the LORD, "My refuge and my fortress, my God, in whom I trust"

(Psalm 91:1-2, NASB). Does this mean we will never suffer from the attack of those controlled by Satan? No, there are times that bad things happen to good people.

Many things we will never understand, but we know that our God is present with us at all times. "The LORD is your keeper; the LORD is your shade on your right hand" (Psalm 121:5, NASB).We can find rest in the protection of our Lord. A mother hen gathers her chicks under her wing for protection and the Lord also offers protection for us under his wing. "He will cover you with His pinions, and under His wings you may seek refuge; His faithfulness is a shield and bulwark" (Psalm 91:4, NASB). We are blessed by God who loves us as His children and desires to protect us at all times.

When tornadoes and thunderstorms come, people are very frightened by the storms. They seek cover and protection in storm shelters. God offers shelter to Christians when they encounter the storms of life. They can find comfort in the scripture and also through encouragement from other believers. Mama hens scurry around and gather their baby chicks under their wings when a predator is around. A mama cow will run at you if she thinks you are going to bother her new baby calf. Airlines now have heavy security to protect their passengers because of terrorism in our world. Almost everywhere we go; we can see some type of protection that is in force for the citizens of our land. The greatest protection we can have is to know that we are saved and when we die we will go to heaven to live forever with the Lord. God inspired men to write the Bible in order that we could know that we have eternal life. "I have written these things to you who believe in the name of the Son of God, so that you may know that you have eternal life" (1John 5:13, HCSB).

God's Chosen Messenger

My mom told me about one of her cousins who was called to preach. It was difficult for him because he could not read. He loved the Lord and he was determined to preach the Word of God. On the Saturday, before he would preach on Sunday, his wife would read him the passage of scripture he would be using the next day. Even though he could not read, he had a very sharp memory. She would read the scripture over and over to him and by Sunday morning, he could almost quote the passage by memory. He had a hunger, an urgent desire, to learn more about the Lord and he was able to do this with the help of his wife. It seems that when a person is limited in what he can do that God empowers him in other areas. He wanted so much to be pleasing to God. When the heart is soft and moldable, God can do amazing things with a person who is determined to speak for Him. "Let the words of my mouth and the meditation of my heart be acceptable in Thy sight, O Lord, my rock and my Redeemer" (Psalm 19:14, NASB). This verse could have easily been the prayer of his heart.

John the Baptist was sent by God to prepare the way for Jesus as He came in human form. "There came a man, sent from God, whose name was John. He came for a witness, that he might bear witness of the light, that all might believe through him. He was not the light, but came that he might bear witness of the light. There was the true light which, coming into the world, enlightens every man" (John 1:6-9, NASB). John was an unusual man who certainly did not receive any schooling. He simply delivered the message that God gave him to speak. "Now John himself had a garment of camel's hair, and a leather belt about his waist; and his food was locusts and wild honey." (Matthew 3:4, NASB). God sent him for a very special purpose. "As for me, I baptize you with water for repentance, but He who is coming after me is mightier than I, and I am not fit to remove His sandals; He will baptize you with the Holy Spirit and fire" (Matthew 3:11, NASB).

God called Ezekiel to go and deliver His message to the house of Israel. He did not send him out without proper instruction. He told him exactly what to do.

> Then He said to me, "Son of man, eat what you find; eat this scroll and go speak to the house of Israel." So I opened my mouth, and He fed me this scroll. And He said to me, "Son of man, feed your stomach, and fill your body with this scroll which I am giving you," Then I ate it, and it was sweet as honey in my mouth.
>
> Ezekiel 3:1-3 (NASB)

God told Ezekiel that the house of Israel would not listen to Him and neither would they listen to Ezekiel. They were a stubborn and obstinate people.

> Moreover, He said to me, "Son of man, take into your heart all My words which I shall speak to you, and listen closely. And go to the

> exiles, to the sons of your people, and speak to them and tell them, whether they listen or not, 'Thus says the Lord God.'"
>
> Ezekiel 3:10-11 (NASB)

God's message was to be proclaimed whether they listened or not. Ezekiel was a willing vessel for the Lord.

My mother's cousin was willing to do whatever it took to learn the Word of God so he could be used by God to deliver His message. John the Baptist was a man that lived out in the desert. He dressed differently than everyone else and ate some things that were strange, but God used him to prepare the way for Jesus. Ezekiel had a hunger for the Word of God and when he ate it, it was sweeter than honey in his mouth. His message was not a popular message, but God told him that Israel would refuse to listen but he was to preach to them anyway. What about you? Are you willing to go and teach or preach for the Lord even though you may not feel adequate to do what God desires of you? All he asks is that you commit your life to Him, allow Him to prepare you for the task ahead and that you serve Him with all your heart.

The Blowing of the Wind

In 2009, my husband and I went to Borger, Texas. Traveling through Weatherford and Sayre, Oklahoma where there is an abundance of wind, we were amazed at the number of windmill generators we saw. They produced electrical current that was fed into the lines for the Public Service of Oklahoma that provided electricity for surrounding towns. The blades of the windmills appeared so small until you passed a semi-truck pulling a flatbed trailer with one blade on it. They were actually around sixty feet long. The generators on top of the windmills looked small, but they were larger than a car engine. In these areas, it is very windy and the winds cause the blades to turn, thereby, producing electricity. The wind is very useful in these areas.

Sometimes the wind can be very dangerous. I have been out in a boat on a lake fishing when the wind was blowing and it was very frightening as the wind caused the water to churn, causing large waves. The waves became so strong that they caused our boat to be tossed around. We had to get to shore as quickly as we could. In this situation, the wind causes unusual things to happen.

Jesus had just performed the miracle of the feeding of the five thousand with only five loaves of bread and two small fish. He instructed His disciples to get into the boat and go ahead of Him to the other side of the Sea of Galilee. Jesus then went up on the mountain by himself to pray. "When evening came, He was there alone. But the boat was already over a mile from land, battered by the waves, because the wind was against them" (Matthew 14:23b-24, HCSB). The scripture tells us that Jesus came walking toward the disciples on the sea. The disciples were frightened because they thought it was a ghost. "Immediately Jesus spoke to them. "Have courage! It is I. Don't be afraid"" (Matthew 14:27, HCSB). Peter said if it was Jesus, He should tell him to walk to Him on the water. ""Come!" He said. And climbing out of the boat, Peter started walking on the water and came toward Jesus. But when he saw the strength of the wind, he was afraid. And beginning to sink he cried out, "Lord, save me"" (Matthew 14:29-30, HCSB). The wind caused the water to be rough, but as long as Peter kept his eyes on Jesus and did not pay attention to the wind, he was able to walk on water to Jesus. But, Peter observed what the wind was doing to the water and he began to sink. The scripture tells us that Jesus reached out His hand to Peter and caught him. "When they got into the boat, the wind ceased" (Matthew 14:32, HCSB). Before Jesus arrived, the boat was being tossed to and fro by the wind and waves. When Jesus calmed the waters, all who were in the boat worshipped the Son of God. Jesus has the power to control the wind that causes the water of a lake or sea to be rough.

When the wind is used to generate electricity for homes around the area, it is a good thing. On a hot day the gentle blowing of the wind can bring relief from the heat. If we are out on a body of water and the winds come up, it is a dangerous situation as it causes the boat to toss to and fro. The Lord Jesus can calm the wind and waves and He is able to bring peace and calm to every situation in our lives. We allow ourselves to get tangled in the problems of life and forget to trust the Lord to bring peace. When you are buffeted about by the blowing of the wind, how do you respond? Our immediate response is fear, but we must remember that God promises to be with us at all times. If you do not know the promises of God, purchase a little book of God's promises and memorize some of them so you can quote the scriptures when you are afraid. Whether it is fear, anxiety, questions about whether God answers prayers, problems in your family or many other topics, the Bible contains promises from the Lord of His provision during these times. Do you see God in the midst of all that is happening in your life? When good things happen in our lives, many times we do not give God the credit. We say that it just happened by accident. Things do not happen to a believer just by accident because God is always at work in our lives. Give Him the credit and thank Him for what He did. When we allow God to be in the midst of all that is going on in our lives, we trust in Him to do whatever is needed in every aspect of our lives. Do you pause to pray and ask for God's help to get you through the trying situations of life? Jesus said; "In the world you have tribulation, but take courage; I have overcome the world" (John 16:33b, NASB).

An Unbearable Burden of Sin

When I was a child, I could not stand for my parents to be upset with me. If I had done something wrong sooner or later I would admit it to my folks, because I did not want them to be disappointed in me because of my disobedience. It would continually weigh on my mind, gnawing on my conscience.

Our youngest son was the same way. It wore heavily on his mind if he thought we knew about what he had done. If I questioned him about a situation, he was sure I knew the wrong he had committed. It might be a day, a week, a month, or even a year, but sooner or later he would admit to his wrongdoing. He would be so relieved when he admitted to what he had done. It was like an unbearable burden had been lifted off his shoulders.

The Israelites seemed to be chronic complainers as they journeyed from Egypt to the promised land. There were times that God's patience wore thin and He brought down judgment upon them.

> NOW the people became like those who complain of adversity in the hearing of the LORD; and when the LORD heard it, His anger was kindled, and the fire of the LORD burned among them and consumed some of the out-

> skirts of the camp. The people therefore cried out to Moses, and Moses prayed to the LORD, and the fire died out.
>
> Numbers 11:1-2 (NASB)

Some of the foreigners who had joined them in their travel began to complain about the food and the Israelites joined in. God had given them manna to eat, but yet, they were not satisfied. They began to think of the fish, melons, cucumbers, leeks, onions, and garlic they ate in Egypt and they began to grumble and complain.

Moses felt the burden of these obstinate people who were never satisfied. He cried out to God.

> Now Moses heard the people weeping throughout their families, each man at the doorway of his tent; and the anger of the LORD was kindled greatly, and Moses was displeased. So Moses said to the LORD, "Why hast Thou been so hard on Thy servant? And why have I not found favor in Thy sight, that thou has laid the burden of all this people on me?"
>
> Numbers 11:10-11 (NASB)

Moses inquired of the Lord concerning how much he was going to need to do for these people. He asked the Lord where he was going to get meat and then he asked the Lord to give them meat so they could eat. "I alone am not able to carry all these people, because it is too burdensome for me" (Numbers 11:14, NASB). Moses even went so far as to ask the Lord to kill him if he was deserving of God's favor. We know from the story of Israel's wilderness journey that they complained the whole way. When there was lack of water, lack of bread, lack of meat, or if Moses stayed on the mountain too long, the people complained and wanted to take matters in their own hands. Moses cried out to God asking Him to please relieve him of this burden.

If we have a deep seated love for the Lord, sin we have committed will wear heavily upon our mind and heart. It will eat away at our conscience and the convicting power of the Lord will come upon us. Jesus had eaten the last supper with the disciples and was speaking to them about their falling away from Him. Peter said that others might fall away from Him, but he would never fall away. Jesus told him that before the cock crowed, he would deny him three times. Peter boldly said that he would never deny the Lord. When Jesus was taken before Caiaphas, the high priest, Peter followed and was out in the courtyard. Three different times he was questioned concerning his connection with Jesus and three times he denied that he was one of Jesus's followers.

> Then he started to curse and to swear with an oath, "I do not know the man!" Immediately a rooster crowed, and Peter remembered the words Jesus had spoken, "Before the rooster crows, you will deny Me three times." And he went outside and wept bitterly.
>
> Matthew 26:74-75 (HCSB)

Peter realized what he had done when he heard the rooster crow. He was convicted of the sin he had committed and he ran away and wept bitterly. His sin wore heavily upon him.

We know that Jesus forgave Peter of his sin of denying that he knew Him because Peter was one of the first ones that Jesus appeared to after His resurrection. In the gospel of John, Jesus questioned Peter concerning whether or not he loved Him. He then told him to tend to His sheep. Jesus was restoring the relationship between Him and Peter. My parents forgave me as I also forgave my son, but we still had to endure the consequences. God will lift the burden of sin if we will confess our sin to Him. He loves us in spite of our sin.

Chosen by God to Be a Great Example

My greatest example in life has been my dear mother who entered heaven's gates in March of 2005. Mom was a real mentor to me and taught me by the life that she lived. She set the example for me as to the way I was to care for my own family. Most of all, my mom was a great spiritual leader and advisor to me. She loved the Lord and treasured His word. She instilled in me the desire to know the Lord more fully through the study of His word. When I think of Mother, my thoughts go to the verses found in the book of Psalm:

> I have set the LORD continually before me; because He is at my right hand, I will not be shaken. Thou wilt make known to me the path of life; in Thy presence is fulness of joy; in Thy right hand there are pleasures forever.
>
> Psalm 16:8, 11 (NASB)

Mom depended on the Lord in every aspect of her life. She did not become anxious and go about wringing her hands, but she prayed, seeking His companionship and guidance in her life.

Elijah was a great prophet of God. The time came for Elijah to be taken into heaven to be with the Father. Elisha, who was also a prophet, accompanied Elijah to Gilgal. Before Elijah was taken up, he took his successor with him to three different places.

> And Elijah said to Elisha, "Stay here please, for the Lord has sent me as far as Bethel." But Elisha said, "As the Lord lives and as you yourself live, I will not leave you." So they went down to Bethel. Then the sons of the prophets who were at Bethel came out to Elisha and said to him. "Do you know that the Lord will take away your master from over you today?" And he said "Yes, I know; be still."
>
> 2 Kings 2:2-3 (NASB)

They went through this same situation two other times as Elijah journeyed to Jericho and to the Jordan River. Each time Elijah encouraged Elisha to stay in the place where they were, but Elisha was determined to accompany Elijah to every destination. An amazing thing happened at the Jordan River when Elijah and Elisha needed to cross it.

> And Elijah took his mantle and folded it together and struck the waters, and they were divided here and there, so that the two of them crossed over on dry ground. Now it came about when they had crossed over, that Elijah said to Elisha, "Ask what I shall do for you before I am taken from you." And Elisha said, "Please, let a double portion of your spirit be upon me."
>
> 2 Kings 2:8-9 (NASB)

Elijah told him that the only way this would happen was if he saw him when he was taken up into heaven. Elisha had walked with Elijah and attended to his needs many different times.

The only inheritance Elisha desired was a double measure of his master's inner spirit of courage, his faithfulness, his faith in God, and his obedience to God's will. By saying this, Elisha was accepting the prophetic ministry that Elijah had begun and with God's help he determined to carry it on to completion.

> Then it came about as they were going along and talking, that behold, there appeared a chariot of fire and horses of fire which separated the two of them. And Elijah went up by a whirlwind to heaven. And Elisha saw it and cried out, "My father, my father, the chariots of Israel and its horsemen!" And he saw him no more.
>
> 2 Kings 2:11-12a (NASB)

Because he saw Elijah translated into heaven, he received a double portion of his spirit.

God chose my mother to be a great example for me to imitate. My greatest desire is to be a dedicated servant of God like my mother. Elijah was a great example for Elisha and he desired to imitate the inner qualities God had instilled in Elijah. What about you? Do you have a person you desire to imitate as you walk with the Lord?

God Speaks—Change Is Evident

One day I drove to Muskogee, Oklahoma, to take materials for a book signing I was going to have. When I drove down Okmulgee Street, God showed me so vividly the beauty of His creation. The street was lined with trees of all different colors. It was evidence of God's amazing creative power. There were red leaves, gold leaves, green leaves, orange leaves, and even some brown leaves. God did not ask me if I wanted Him to change the color of the trees. I believe it was God's purpose in creating the different seasons to show man that all things are possible with the Lord. No artist can sweep across the expanse of our earth and create a masterpiece as beautiful as our Lord does in the changing of the leaves. We could plan for months how we were going to bring this change about and our plans would fail because it is not within our power. But, in God's timing His purpose for all things is accomplished. In the fall of the year, the changing of the color of the leaves makes us realize afresh and anew, "'For my thoughts are not your thoughts, neither are your ways my ways,' declares the LORD" (Isaiah 55:8, NASB).

Throughout the Bible, we have illustrations of God telling man what He was going to do. He did not ask man what he thought he should do.

> And God looked on the earth, and behold, it was corrupt; for all flesh had corrupted their way upon the earth. Then God said to Noah, "The end of all flesh has come before Me; for the earth is filled with violence because of them; and behold, I am about to destroy them with the earth."
>
> Genesis 6:12-13 (NASB)

God did not ask Noah what he thought He should do about the corruption of the people on earth, but He told Noah what He was going to do because of their sin.

In the Old Testament, God used the prophets to deliver His message to the people concerning what was going to happen because of the wickedness in their life and their failure to worship Him. The Lord spoke to Jeremiah about His purpose for forming him in his mother's womb. Even before Jeremiah was born, God had appointed him as a prophet to the nations. Jeremiah began to make excuses as to why he could not do this.

> Then I said, "Alas, Lord GOD! Behold I do not know how to speak, because I am a youth." But the LORD said to me, "Do not say, 'I am a youth,' because everywhere I send you, you shall go, and all that I command you, you shall speak. Do not be afraid of them, for I am with you to deliver you," declares the LORD.
>
> Jeremiah 1:6-8 (NASB)

God did not ask Jeremiah what he thought He should do, but God told Jeremiah exactly how He was going to use him to accomplish His purpose.

Our old human nature causes us to sit around and dream up what we want to do and how we want to accomplish it. This is not God's way of doing things. God desires that we have an intimate relationship with Him. He is not dependent on our plans. He wants us to trust in Him to reveal to us His purpose and be willing to be used by Him to accomplish His purpose. How is your relationship with the Lord? Is it such that you hear God speaking to your innermost being encouraging you to become a part of His work? Listen! God will speak to you through many different avenues, particularly the Bible. The leaves change their color in the fall of the year. How does your character change as the Holy Spirit reveals things to you from God's Word and your relationship grows more intimate?

Walking and Talking with the Lord

I am more consistent in my walking each day for exercise when I am getting ready to make a trip where I will be doing a lot of walking. I know that my legs need to be strong for all the walking we will do. I am not as young as I was when I started making these trips and it does make a difference. The joy I find in walking is that I spend that time memorizing scripture. It is a joy to walk and talk with the Lord each day out in the midst of His beautiful creation. Our home is behind Robbers Cave State Park, so as I walk I look at the hills that surround me. It reminds me of the scripture; "I will lift up my eyes to the mountains; from whence shall my help come? My help comes from the LORD, who made heaven and earth" (Psalm 121:1-2, NASB). As I walk and memorize the scripture, I know that without the Lord I would be weak. He truly is my strength each day. What sweeter words could the Lord hear than to have the scripture spoken to Him?

My parents gave me a Thompson Chain Bible to encourage me to study the Word of God. They encouraged me to continually walk and talk with the Lord. My dad wrote the following words in my Bible:

> We hope you will let this Bible be food for your soul, a comfort when in sorrow, a strength when weak, a guide when tempted to drift, a light to show you God's way, and the source for a successful, happy Christian life and home. Prayerfully yours, Mother and Dad.

My parents directed me to the Word of God, so I would know the meaning of walking and talking with the Lord.

We find examples in the Bible of those who walked in close fellowship with the Lord.

> Enoch walked [in habitual fellowship] with God after the birth of Methuselah 300 years and had other sons and daughters. So all the days of Enoch were 365 years. And Enoch walked [in habitual fellowship] with God; and he was not, for God took him [home with Him].
>
> Genesis 5:22-24 (AMP)

Enoch knew what it was to walk in close fellowship with God. We need to think about our own life and whether or not we are daily in habitual fellowship with the Lord. Do we consider our relationship with the Lord to be an intimate relationship with Him?

> Because of faith Enoch was caught up and transferred to heaven, so that he did not have a glimpse of death; and he was not found, because God had translated him. For even before he was taken to heaven, he received testimony [still on

> record] that he had pleased and been satisfactory to God.
>
> Hebrews 11:5 (AMP)

If God were to evaluate our life today, what kind of report would we get? Would our life be pleasing and satisfactory in the eyes of the Lord?

The Bible tells us that the tribe of Levi was set aside to serve as priests in the temple. Malachi was reprimanding the present priests, because they did not love the Lord as they should and they did not care about being pleasing to the Lord. He reminded them that the tribe of Levi had been faithful to the Lord in the past.

> My covenant with him was one of life and peace, and I gave these to him; it called for reverence, and he revered Me and stood in awe of My name. True instruction was in his mouth, and nothing wrong was found on his lips. He walked with Me in peace and fairness and turned many from sin.
>
> Malachi 2:5-6 (HCSB)

We are to show God the same reverence and respect as He expected from the Levites. We are to live a life of truth walking every step of the way with the Lord.

As we walk and talk with the Lord, our lives will show evidence of that relationship and people will be won to the Lord through our witness. We may never know how many people we have influenced in the way we have walked and talked with the Lord, but the Lord will reap the harvest. Be diligent in serving the Lord today.

The Stain of Sin

The other day I was cleaning my house in preparation for friends who were coming to stay with us a few days. When I cleaned our refrigerator, I took out a jar of pickled beets and a jar of broth I wanted to throw away. My plan was to take the contents of the jars and throw them over the fence into our pasture. I opened the jar of beets and proceeded to try to open the jar of broth. It had been in the refrigerator for some time and the lid was stuck. As I tried to open it, the jar slipped out of my hands, hit the jar of pickled beets and the contents fell on our carpet, which is white with different colored threads in it. My heart sank to my feet as I saw all those beets and a large scarlet stain on the carpet. I immediately began to pick up the beets and spray carpet cleaner on the red stain to try to remove it from the carpet. After using several different cleaners, a brush, and dry rags to soak up the stain, we still have a pink stain on our carpet. I will continue trying to remove the stain.

What happens to the stain of sin in the life of a person when they come to know Jesus as Savior and Lord? "'Come now, and let us reason together,' says the LORD, 'though your sins are as scarlet, they will be as white as snow; though they are red like crimson, they will be like wool'" (Isaiah 1:18, NASB). It must have shocked the people when they heard Isaiah compare the holy city of Jerusalem to Sodom and Gomorrah. The children of Israel were rebellious people, but also a religious people. They came to the temple to worship bringing all types of sacrifices, and yet, their hearts were far from God. Their sacrifices to be placed on the altar and burned were not all that God desired from them. "The sacrifices of God are a broken spirit; a broken and a contrite heart, O God, Thou wilt not despise" (Psalm 51:17, NASB). God desires a humble and repentant heart. We are to be crushed by the sense of guilt and sinfulness in our life.

In Isaiah 1:18, the word *reason* means "to decide a case in court," but instead of pronouncing judgment, the judge offered pardon. They needed to cleanse themselves by repenting and turning away from sin. If they would repent, they would be cleansed of their sin. A scarlet stain is almost impossible to remove from clothing or carpet, but the Bible says that even though our sins are as scarlet, they will become as white as a new fallen snow or as white as the wool of sheep. Through the blood that Jesus shed upon the cross, we can be cleansed of our sin. We must place our faith and trust in Jesus who is the light of the world. We are to no longer walk in the darkness of sin but in Jesus, the light of the world. "…but if we walk in the light as He Himself is in the light, we have fellowship with one another, and the blood of Jesus His Son cleanses us from all sin" (1 John 1:7, NASB).

It is possible that I may not completely get the red stain out of my carpet. I know for certain that when

Jesus shed His blood on the cross, was buried and arose from the grave on the third day that all of us were given the opportunity to be forgiven of our sin and receive eternal life. As a child, I realized I was a sinner and I asked God to forgive me of my sin. I was cleansed of my sin at that very moment. I died to my old sinful life and began a new life of walking with Jesus. The Bible tells us that when a born again believer dies, they will be taken to heaven to live with the Lord forever. Have you asked the Lord to wash the stain of sin out of your life by forgiving you of your sin?

Acts of Nature

In the year 2011, we have experienced many acts of nature that have been devastating to people around us. The country of Japan experienced an underwater earthquake, which caused a mighty tidal wave called a tsunami. Many lives were lost, homes and businesses destroyed, and nuclear plants endangered. Oklahoma, Arkansas, Alabama, and Missouri have experienced tornadoes that have taken lives and destroyed property. Alabama had ninety-nine tornadoes touch down on April 27th. The Mississippi River floodwater crest may come very close to the all time high of 48.7 inches. Many homes, businesses, and much farmland have been destroyed by the flooding. We never know when our time on earth will end. The people involved in these acts of nature did not know they were going to happen. We must be sure that we are in right relationship with Jesus Christ and have the assurance that we will spend eternity with Him in heaven when we die.

In the book of Joel, we have the story of the locust invasion that devastated the land of Judah. Because of their sin, God sent the locusts to devour the land. "What the gnawing locust has left, the swarming locust has eaten; and what the swarming locust has left, the creeping locust has eaten; and what the creeping locust left, the stripping locust has eaten" (Joel 1:4, NASB).

Joel was a prophet and he proclaimed the implications of this catastrophe. He described the plague of insects in terms of a human army who after attacking would leave behind devastation. The invading army would be like a swarm of locusts in number. One commentator said that it was more than likely four different swarms of locust. Each group of locusts would destroy what the other one had left. A swarm of locust can very quickly destroy the vegetation of the countryside.

Because of the devastation there were no grapes to make wine. During that time bread and wine were staples in the Jewish diet. The locusts had attacked the vines and the fig trees. It was important socially to have your own vineyard and fig trees in those days. Joel preached to the people asking them to repent of their sin and turn back to God and possibly God would withhold further judgment.

> Consecrate a fast, proclaim a solemn assembly; gather the elders and all the inhabitants of the land to the house of the LORD your God, and cry out to the LORD. Alas for the day! For the day of the LORD is near, and it will come as destruction from the Almighty.
>
> Joel 1:14-15 (NASB)

The day of the Lord was judgment that would come for their sin. God was not content with just outward acts of repentance. There must be true sorrow and repentance that demonstrated a change of heart and sorrow for their sin.

Many different acts of nature are destroying lands, houses, businesses, and people, but it seems that America and other nations are not seeing these acts as warnings from the Lord. Why do we not see these acts of nature as God's warning of worse destruction to come if we do not turn from our sinful ways? All Christians must join together and pray for the forgiveness of their own personal sin and also the sin of our nation.

> "Yet even now," declares the LORD, "return to Me with all your heart, and with fasting, weeping, and mourning; and rend your heart and not your garments." Now return to the LORD your God, for He is gracious and compassionate, slow to anger, abounding in loving kindness, and relenting of evil.
>
> Joel 2:12-13 (NASB)

We must listen to what God is saying to us and heed His warning. The Bible is very applicable to our lives today. We have many things happening in our world today that are much the same as things that happened in biblical times. If God disapproved of them then, He still disapproves today. We neglect the study of the Bible so much in our lives that we have no idea what God's Word says about things we are facing. Complacency has engulfed our lives. When we read about what God did in biblical times concerning the rebellious spirits of His people, a red flag should go up when we realize that it is happening today. This should act as a warning to us that we need to pray and ask God how we can help change things in our world or possibly it may be something in our personal life. God speaks to us by the Holy Spirit through His word, prayer, God's people and different circumstances in our life. In order for us to hear God speak to us, we must learn to sit quietly before Him, pray and seek His direction. Get away from the busyness of life because it will be a distraction in hearing God speak. Get alone with the Lord because He is waiting to hear from you. There are times when we are listening to gospel music that God may speak to us through the words of a song. "On the day I called Thou didst answer me; Thou didst make me bold with strength in my soul" (Psalm 138:3, NASB).

I Surrender

Growing up, I was always a tomboy. I was not afraid of the boys or what they could do to me. I was just as tough as they were and I hit as hard as they did in football and could hit a baseball as far as they did. I spent most of my time playing the games that the boys played. Many times we would wrestle and scuffle around. When it seemed that one had got the best of the other, the one on the bottom would usually holler, “I've had enough. I surrender.” What they really meant was they wanted the one on top to get off of them so they could get up. It also meant you were giving up, surrendering to them, declaring them as the winner of the fight.

In many of the westerns like Gunsmoke, we have seen the bad guy under fire by Marshall Dillon. When he realizes there is no way he can win the battle, he may throw out his gun and say, "I surrender" or he may tie a white flag on the end of his rifle and hold it in the air showing that he is surrendering.

Surrender is the act of giving up or giving the possession of something to another. In essence, this is what the bad guy is doing when he says, "I surrender."

What are the characteristics of a life totally surrendered to God? It will be a life that is totally consecrated to the Lord. To be consecrated means to be set apart for God, to be kept or used for a special purpose. It is the act of yielding oneself to the control of the Lord. "My son, give me your heart, and let your eyes observe my ways" (Proverbs 23:26, HCSB). For us to be fully consecrated to the Lord, we need to allow the Lord to have full control of our heart. We strive to fill our heart with things of the Lord rather than things of the world. We seek wisdom from the Lord. Our daily prayer should be as David wrote in the book of Psalm, "Create in me a clean heart, O God, and renew a steadfast spirit within me" (Psalm 51:10, NASB).

The scribes and Pharisees held to the traditions of their elders. They were condemning the disciples because they did not wash their hands before they ate bread. Jesus mentioned to them that they went against the commandments of God for the sake of their tradition. Jesus continued teaching His followers about these traditions. "This people honors me with their lips, but their heart is far away from me. Not what enters into the mouth defiles the man, but what proceeds out of the mouth, this defiles man" (Matthew 15:8, 11, NASB). Jesus emphasized with His followers that whatever was in the heart was what would come out of the mouth. Much is said about the condition of the heart in the scripture and how it affects what a believer does. "For as he thinks in his heart, so is he" (Proverbs 23:7a, AMP). We are to be set apart from the world and think on things of God.

If we want to live a surrendered life to the Lord, we will no longer have the desire to sin.

> For we know that our old self was crucified with Him in order that sin's dominion over the body

> may be abolished, so that we may no longer be enslaved to sin, since a person who has died is freed from sin's claims. Now if we died with Christ, we believe that we will also live with Him…
>
> Romans 6:6-8 (HCSB)

It does not mean we will never sin again, but the desire of our heart changed when we came to know Jesus.

The desire of our heart will be to live our life in the will of God. "I delight to do Your will, my God; Your instruction resides within me" (Psalm 40:8, HCSB). We must study God's Word and allow it to infiltrate every inch of our heart. As we learn the teachings of the Lord, He instills in us the desire to live our life in the center of His will and purpose for our life. What is the desire of your heart? Can you say with assurance, "I surrender all that I am and ever hope to be to the Lord"?

Persistent Faith

The other day as we were traveling there was a quote on a church sign that got my attention. The quote was, "Faith is the postage stamp on our prayers." Thinking about this statement reminded me that without faith our prayers are of no avail.

The story was told to me about a woman living somewhere around Oklahoma City that was a persistent prayer warrior. One day as she was praying for a friend, God told her to go and purchase a blue Bible for her friend. She went to a Christian bookstore and asked for a blue Bible in the King James Version. The clerk informed her that they did not have a blue Bible. She left disappointed that they did not have the Bible she needed. She stopped and thought about the fact that God had told her as she prayed to give her friend this particular color of Bible. She turned around and went back to the store. Once again the clerk said they did not have a blue Bible. She told her that she had to have one, because God had told her to come get it for this person. Probably by this time the clerk was a little irritated with the woman, but the woman persisted. The top shelf in the store had many new Bibles stacked on it and she pointed to a particular place and asked the clerk to see if there was a blue Bible in that box. Sure enough, when the clerk opened the box there was a blue King James Version of the Bible. As she prayed that morning, God had shown her what she needed to do. She had faith that what God had purposed would happen. "Therefore, I tell you, all the things you pray and ask for — believe that you have received them, and you will have them" (Mark 11:24, HCSB). What good does it do us to pray if we do not have the faith that God will hear our prayer and accomplish what He reveals to us? A letter cannot go anywhere without a postage stamp and neither will God hear and answer our prayers if we do not have faith.

In the gospels of Matthew, Mark, and Luke, we have the story of a woman who showed persistent faith. Jesus had just crossed Lake Galilee and many people were gathered around him. "A woman suffering from bleeding for 12 years had endured much under many doctors. She had spent everything she had and was not helped at all. On the contrary, she became worse" (Mark 5:25-26, HCSB). The woman was destitute without any money and still suffering from her affliction. According to the law, she was ceremonially unclean and this restricted her religious and social life. She had a very heavy burden to bear, but then she heard that Jesus was in the area. "Having heard about Jesus, she came behind Him in the crowd and touched His robe. For she said, "If I can just touch His robes, I'll be made well" (Mark 5:27-28, HCSB)! It probably took all the strength she could muster to go to where Jesus was, but she had faith that she would be made well. "Instantly her flow of blood ceased, and she sensed in her body that she was cured of her affliction" (Mark 5:29, HCSB).

Jesus realized that power had gone from His body and He asked who had touched Him. The disciples were amazed that Jesus would ask this question with all the people pressing in around Him. The woman came and fell at His feet admitting that she was the one who touched Him. ""Daughter," He said to her, "your faith has made you well. Go in peace and be free from your affliction"" (Mark 5:34, HCSB).

When we truly believe and place our faith in the Lord, we will recognize God's amazing work all around us. The Bible tells us that if we pray in accordance with God's will that He will answer our prayers. The woman in Oklahoma City believed God told her to purchase a blue Bible for her friend. I do not doubt that it was God's will for her to give a Bible to her friend and she had the faith to search for a blue Bible. "Faith is the postage stamp on our prayers."

The Early Morning Jump Start

One of the joys of living in the country is that you have all types of little creatures running around. The one that adapts really well to our house is a mouse. When we see one scurrying about our home, the first thing we do is set a mouse trap. Years ago when our youngest son, Stevie, was still home I discovered that we had a mouse in a trap. I was in the midst of making biscuits for breakfast when Stevie woke up and stumbled into the kitchen. I asked him if he would take the trap outside and get rid of the mouse. He was still half asleep and as he reached down to pick up the trap with the mouse in it, the mouse jumped because he still had a little life in him. Stevie was a big boy, tall in stature and very strong, but this little mouse scared him half to death. You talk about getting an early morning jump start, Stevie did. You would have thought he had seen a ghost.

How do we get an early morning jump start as a born again believer? Jesus set the example in the way that He arose early in the morning to go off by Himself to pray. "And in the early morning, while it was still dark, He arose and went out and departed to a lonely place, and was praying there." (Mark 1:35, NASB). Jesus realized the importance of beginning His day in prayer to God the Father. If it was that important to Jesus, why is it not important to all of us? The best jump start for our day is time spent alone with the Lord not only speaking to Him but listening and allowing Him to speak to us.

Another necessity in getting an early morning jump start with the Lord is to spend time in the Word of God. I get up very early in the morning to spend time with the Lord because there is no noise whatsoever, except maybe a cricket or the sound of an animal outside. I know no one is going to interrupt my time with the Lord. "Jesus therefore was saying to those Jews who had believed Him, 'If you abide in My word, then you are truly disciples of Mine; and you shall know the truth and the truth shall make you free'" (John 8:31-32, NASB). If we are truly a child of God, we will have a desire to spend time with Jesus in His Word.

Think about your life as a believer and the fact that sometimes things do not go as they should. It seems that you just cannot get things going in the right direction for that day. Perhaps you had decided that you must get up earlier in the morning so you could spend time with the Lord, but when the alarm went off, you rolled over and went back to sleep. Why do you think your day was not going as it should? "All Scripture is given by inspiration of God, and is profitable for doctrine, for reproof, for correction, for instruction in righteousness, that the man of God may be complete, thoroughly equipped for every good work" (2 Timothy 3:16-17, NKJV). Sometimes people do not like to read the Word of God because it has strong, convicting power. We do not like to be confronted with the sin in our life. Good intentions are great if we fulfill them. It must not be just a head commitment, but it must be a commitment of the heart. If you make an appointment with a doctor, you keep it. Why are we so negligent in keeping our daily appointment with the Lord?

Stevie was scared half to death when he had his early morning jump start with the mouse moving. Our jump start for the day should bring joy to our heart when we spend time with the Lord in prayer and in His word. We come away with our cup filled to overflowing and determined to be a good witness for the Lord. Make an appointment. Set your alarm clock. Get out of bed immediately, wash your face and make yourself presentable. Go alone by yourself, read God's Word, and talk with Him in prayer. It may be for fifteen minutes the first day, but I guarantee you that you will want to increase that length of time when you see how it will change your life.

The Mighty Force of the Wind

As I gazed out the window of my study this morning, I could see the wind blowing briskly through the trees. It reminded me of a fishing trip I went on with my father-in-law in California. We were in the mountains above San Bernardino, California, on Big Bear Lake in an aluminum fishing boat when the clouds began getting very dark. Soon, the wind began to blow and it was tossing our boat around. We decided it was time for us to try to make it to shore. We did not have a motor on the boat, so we had to row the boat. It was very difficult, because the wind was so strong. All the time the sky was getting darker and darker and it looked like rain was on its way. By the time we managed to get the boat to shore, it was beginning to rain. How thankful we were to be off of the lake, out of the boat, and on solid ground!

Jesus had spent the day teaching the many people that were following Him. When evening came, He told the disciples to get in the boat and go to the other side of the Sea of Galilee. Jesus was in the boat with them.

> And there arose a fierce gale of wind, and the waves were breaking over the boat so much that the boat was already filling up. And He Himself was in the stern, asleep on the cushion; and they

> awoke Him and said to Him, "Teacher, do You not care that we are perishing?"
>
> Mark 4:37-38 (NASB)

The disciples were afraid as the mighty force of the wind was tossing their boat around. The waves coming over the side of the boat were filling it with water. Jesus was asleep in the stern of the boat and they were probably bewildered as to how Jesus could sleep in the midst of such a storm. They awoke Jesus asking Him if He was not concerned that they were perishing.

Jesus may have been a little upset with them when they awoke Him from a much needed rest, but He did an amazing thing. "And being aroused, He rebuked the wind and said to the sea, 'Hush, be still.' And the wind died down and it became perfectly calm" (Mark 4:39, NASB). Probably the disciples were in awe of what Jesus had done, but Jesus asked them a question that we all should take note of. "And He said to them, 'Why are you so timid? How is it that you have no faith?'" (Mark 4:40, NASB). Jesus questioned the condition of their faith and why it was that they had not demonstrated their faith as the strong winds were coming against the boat. They had been walking with Jesus, living with Him, and listening to His instruction for their lives day after day. Why did they get so alarmed when Jesus was right there in the boat with them? There are times we take our eyes off of Jesus and we look at things from a human point of view. We forget God's promise that He will never leave us nor will He ever forsake us.

They still did not understand all about Jesus and what He was saying to them. "And they became very much afraid and said to one another, 'Who then is this, that even the wind and the sea obey Him?'" (Mark 4:41, NASB). They still had much to learn about their Master even though they had been with Him for some time.

When we go through stressful situations, whether out on a body of water or just in our every day routine of life, Jesus can bring peace to the situation if we will call on Him. He will come in the midst of our difficulties and say, "Hush, be still." He desires that we come quietly to Him seeking the peace that only He can give us in our life. Be still before the Lord today and ask Him to bring peace and calm in whatever circumstances you are experiencing. The mighty force of the winds blowing in your life will calm down and you will realize that God is right there with you in the midst of every storm you face. "Be still, and know that I am God..." (Psalm 46:10a, NKJV).

Tattered and Worn

The other day as we were traveling a church sign caught my attention. It read, "If your Bible is falling apart, chances are your life is staying together." As I thought about this statement, God helped me to see the truth of these words. When we spend our time reading and meditating on God's Word, our Bible is evidence to others that it is being used continually. The cover may be tattered and worn and the pages may be wrinkled from constant use or stained by tears that may fall when we are convicted by the Word of God. Our daily living is our greatest evidence that we have spent time with the Lord studying the scripture. Our life is an expression of the joy found in being well acquainted with the author of the Bible. Trials may come into our life, but we must trust the Lord to see us through.

God's Word is the most powerful weapon we have as believers.

> For the Word that God speaks is alive and full of power [making it active, operative, energizing, and effective]; it is sharper than any two-edged sword, penetrating to the dividing line of the breath of life (soul) and [the immortal] spirit, and of joints and marrow [of the deepest parts of our nature], exposing and sifting and

> analyzing and judging the very thoughts and purposes of the heart.
>
> Hebrews 4:12 (AMP)

I am thankful for the Holy Spirit who helps me to understand more clearly what God is saying to me as I read the Bible. The teaching of the Lord was given to expose the sin in our life. "For no flesh will be justified in His sight by the works of the law, for through the law comes the knowledge of sin" (Romans 3:20, HCSB).

An angel of the Lord told Philip to go on the desert road that led from Jerusalem to Gaza. As he traveled this road, he met an Ethiopian eunuch who was in charge of the treasury of Candace, queen of the Ethiopians. He had been worshipping in Jerusalem and as he was traveling home he was reading the book of Isaiah the prophet.

> And the Spirit said to Philip, "Go up and join this chariot." And when Philip had run up, he heard him reading Isaiah the prophet, and said, "Do you understand what you are reading?" And he said, "Well, how could I, unless someone guides me?" And he invited Philip to come up and sit with him.
>
> Acts 8:29-31 (NASB)

The eunuch was reading the following verse, "He was oppressed and He was afflicted, yet He did not open His mouth; like a lamb that is led to slaughter, and like a sheep that is silent before its shearers, so He did not open His mouth" (Isaiah 53:7, NASB). The eunuch asked Philip to please explain to him who Isaiah was talking about. He wanted to know if he was talking about himself or someone else. "And Philip opened his mouth, and beginning from this Scripture he preached Jesus to him" (Acts 8:35, NASB). As Philip spoke to him from the scripture, the Ethiopian eunuch began to understand the gospel, because the Holy Spirit was opening his mind to God's truth. He had to understand the scripture to be saved. The eunuch believed and seeing a body of water, he wanted to be baptized. "And Philip said, 'If you believe with all your heart, you may.' And he answered and said, 'I believe that Jesus Christ is the Son of God'" (Acts 8:37, NASB). They stopped the chariot and he was baptized demonstrating his new found faith in Jesus Christ. God's Word has convicting power.

Have you searched the scriptures so much that your Bible is tattered and worn? Through the years, I have seen Bibles that have been read so much by people that the cover was literally coming apart and was definitely tattered and worn. As I looked in their Bible, the pages were wrinkled from use and possibly stained with tears. I knew this Bible had been used consistently through the years. Their lives also demonstrated the time they had spent with the Lord because they had joy in their hearts, a smile on a weather beaten face and a hope because they knew they would spend eternity in heaven with the Lord. They definitely lived their life according to the teachings of the Lord. Does your life show that you have spent much time cultivating your relationship with the Lord through the study of His word? When we have spent time in God's Word, we will know the scriptures. People will know we have spent time in the Bible when we have memorized verses from the Bible. You can tell when a verse has great meaning to that particular person.

Bubbling Over

Many years ago I was baking a red velvet cake from scratch. Now, for you younger ones who do not understand the term "from scratch" that means that you add each ingredient to make the cake. You do not get the cake from a box. I mixed all the ingredients together and put the batter in three round cake pans. I placed them in the oven to bake, set my timer, and went about my work. When I came back to check on how the cake was doing, I could not believe my eyes. It looked like a volcano erupting in my oven, because all of the pans were bubbling over. To this day, I do not know if I did something wrong mixing the batter or if the soda used was overly powerful. Needless to say, the cake was ruined. Think about these pans bubbling over in relation to what would happen in our world today if Christians were bubbling over with the love of Jesus in their hearts.

Paul and Silas went to Philippi to spend some time preaching and teaching. They went down by the riverbank on the Sabbath day supposing that there would be a place of prayer there. They sat down and began to teach the women who were there. Lydia opened her heart to receive Jesus and many members of her household were saved. She entreated Paul and Silas to come and spend some time in her home.

On another day, Paul and Silas were walking to the place of prayer and a slave girl that was demon-possessed and earned money for her master as a fortune-teller kept bothering them. "As she followed Paul and us she cried out, "These men are the slaves of the Most High God, who are proclaiming to you the way of salvation" (Acts 16:17, HCSB). Paul became so annoyed at what she was doing that he turned and commanded the demon to come out of her in the name of Jesus. Paul and Silas ended up being thrown in prison because the owner was so upset that he had lost his source of income.

Paul and Silas were beaten and thrown into prison.

> "About midnight Paul and Silas were praying and singing hymns to God, and the prisoners were listening to them. Suddenly there was such a violent earthquake that the foundations of the jail were shaken, and immediately all the doors were opened, and everyone's chains came loose."
>
> Acts 16:25-26 (HCSB)

Paul and Silas were praying and singing hymns in spite of being in chains. When the earthquake caused the jailer to awaken from his sleep, he saw the prison doors open. Assuming that the prisoners had escaped and knowing what his punishment would be for letting the prisoners escape, he drew his sword to kill himself. Paul shouted to the guard to do himself no harm because they were all there. The other prisoners who were listening to Paul and Silas pray and sing praises to the Lord did not flee from the prison. The jailer came to the dungeon where Paul and Silas were and fell down on his knees before them. "Then he escorted them out and said, "Sirs, what must I do to be saved?" So they said, "Believe on the Lord Jesus, and you will be saved—you and your household"" (Acts 16:30-31, HCSB). Because of their witness, many were saved. The jailer was excited and he took them out and washed their wounds. He took them to his house and set a meal before them. All in his house rejoiced because they had all believed in God.

What would happen if you went around singing songs of praise to the Lord and if you prayed for others as the opportunity came? Do you think it would make a difference in our world? If we continually cultivate our relationship with the Lord by spending time with Him, we will be bubbling over with the joy of our salvation. Try it and see what happens in the lives of people around you. When I went into a store the other day, I was in a happy mood as I had been listening to the Bible being read as I traveled. As I went to the checkout stand, I had a smile on my face and I visited with the checker and inquired about how she was doing. I showed an interest in her life and spoke words of encouragement to her. It was amazing how her whole countenance changed. My red velvet cake bubbled over the edge of the cake pans and covered the bottom of the oven. When we allow the Holy Spirit to have control of our lives, we will be bubbling over and be excited about sharing Jesus with the lost.

Look What I Have!

My favorite picture of my dad is with him holding a big bass that weighed around six to seven pounds. This was his prize catch after a day of fishing. He loved to fish and to catch a fish that large brought joy to his heart. I can just imagine him saying to my mom, "Look what I have!"

I remember when our boys were young and they went to work with their Dad out on construction. Doyal is a concrete contractor, so he is always digging around in the dirt with the backhoe. Of course, when the boys were four and seven they spent time looking for things. One time they came in with something in a bucket and wanted to show me what they had. It was a horny toad they had found on the job. They were excited about their find. Another time they came in with a mole that Doyal had dug up. You never know what boys will bring home. I can still see the excitement on their faces as they said, "Look what we have!"

One night when we were in Malawi serving in missions, I turned back the bedspread on the bed and noticed something black and furry clinging to the back side of the spread. I was not sure what it was so I hollered for Doyal to come look at what was there. As we observed the little creature, we discovered it was a bat. Doyal very hurriedly folded up the bedspread and took it outside and shook the bat off the spread. This does not give you a lot of comfort as you are getting ready to go to bed. Imagine the excitement in my voice as I hollered, "Look what I have!"

Jesus used parables in His teaching to help people understand what He was trying to say. Most of the time a picture speaks louder than words and Jesus tried to help people picture in their minds what he was trying to teach them. When Jesus ate with tax collectors and sinners the scribes and Pharisees criticized Him. Jesus used the illustration of the lost sheep.

> And He told them this parable, saying, "What man among you, if he has a hundred sheep and has lost one of them, does not leave the ninety-nine in the open pasture, and go after the one which is lost, until he finds it? And when he has found it, he lays it on his shoulders, rejoicing. And when he comes home, he calls together his friends and his neighbors, saying to them, 'Rejoice with me, for I have found my sheep which was lost!' I tell you that in the same way, there will be more joy in heaven over one sinner who repents, than over ninety-nine righteous persons who need no repentance."
>
> Luke 15:3-7 (NASB)

Imagine how the shepherd felt when he found out one of his sheep was missing. He began searching for the sheep. The Lord searches for those who are lost that they may know Him.

Some people question why Jesus has not come again with the world in the condition it is in. "The Lord is not slow about His promise, as some count slowness, but is patient toward you, not wishing for any to perish but for all to come to repentance" (2 Peter 3:9, NASB). Jesus is concerned about every lost soul, therefore He delays His coming. He wants every lost person to have the opportunity to repent and come to Him. The angels rejoice when a lost soul is saved. Can't you just hear them saying, "Look what we have! He was lost, but now he is found!"

All of us have probably exclaimed to someone, "Look what I have!" My dad was excited about the fish he caught. The boys were excited about the horny toad and the mole. I was excited when I found the bat clinging to the back side of the bedspread. The shepherd was excited about finding his lost sheep. The angels in heaven rejoice when a lost soul comes to know Jesus. How does it make you feel when you have opportunity to share with someone about Jesus and they pray and ask the Lord to forgive them of their sin and be their Savior and Lord?

The Adventures of a Tongue

The tongue is a very important part of the human body. It enables a person to taste the food they eat. The tongue is used to move food around in our mouth and is a much needed tool for swallowing. Our tongue is used to help us shape the words we speak. To the human, the tongue is a very important instrument.

A frog has a very long tongue and it can reach out and snatch an insect in an instant. The humming bird uses its tongue to suck the nectar from deep within the flower. Moths and butterflies also use their tongues to gather nectar from the flowers. A cow's tongue is extremely rough and quite long. A mama cow uses her tongue to clean the baby calf after it is born. As the cow licks her newborn calf, the rough tongue massages the baby and helps the blood begin to flow through the body. The tongue is very important to insects, birds, and animals.

Once or twice a year we butcher a calf to use as meat. Years ago, when we had a calf butchered, my mom decided to cook the tongue for our family, so we could see if we liked it. They did not waste any part of an animal if it could be eaten when she was a girl. We had never eaten the tongue of a cow before. She baked it like a roast and put a mixture like cherry pie filling on top of it to make it tastier. The tongue had a different texture to it. It did not taste bad, but if our family could use the meat we desired, it would not be our choice. Our dogs enjoyed the delicacy of the tongue since we did not care for it.

What does the Word of God say about the tongue? "If anyone thinks himself to be religious, and yet does not bridle his tongue but deceives his own heart, this man's religion is worthless" (James 1:26, NASB). Many people deceive themselves by talking as if they are believers. They know the proper words to use when they speak and they appear religious, but what they say is not in accordance with the way that they live. James had much to say about the tongue.

> For we all stumble in many ways. If anyone does not stumble in what he says, he is a perfect man, able to bridle the whole body as well. So also the tongue is a small part of the body, and yet it boasts of great things. Behold, how great a forest is set aflame by such a small fire! And the tongue is a fire, the very world of iniquity; the tongue is set among our members as that which defiles the entire body, and sets on fire the course of our life, and is set on fire by hell.
>
> James 3:2, 5-6 (NASB)

When the tongue is used to gossip or to say harsh words to a person, the tongue can be a dangerous tool. It can destroy a person's life when used for bad.

The way a person uses their tongue, the things they say, can infect the whole body. James says that no one can tame the tongue and it can be full of deadly poison.

"With it we bless our Lord and Father; and with it we curse men, who have been made in the likeness of God; from the same mouth come both blessing and cursing. My brethren, these things ought not to be this way" (James 3:9-10, NASB). It is very important that we as believers learn to control our tongues and not use them to speak evil of others.

God desires that we use great wisdom in what we speak. "There is one who speaks rashly like the thrusts of a sword, but the tongue of the wise brings healing. Truthful lips will be established forever, but a lying tongue is only for a moment" (Proverbs 12:18-19, NASB). When we were hurt as children, the loving words of our parents helped bring about healing. Harsh words spoken by a person to another are like a piercing sword. The hurt stays with the other person for a long time.

When the tongue is used to speak encouragement, kindness, and gentle instruction, it is being used as God intended. My mother told me, "If you can't say something good, don't say anything at all." This is wise instruction if we are to honor and glorify the Lord in all we do. Do you need to allow God to control the way you use your tongue?

Abundant Seeds

The pomegranate is the fruit of a bush native to the Middle East and Asia. One can also find pomegranates growing in Africa, India, Malaysia, southern Europe, and in the United States. Pomegranates are grown commercially in Arizona and California. They grow well in mild climates that have little humidity. The season for pomegranates is from October through January of each year.

The inside of a pomegranate will have around seven hundred to eight hundred tightly packed seed casings called arils that are deep red in color when ripe. At first the outside shell of the fruit is a yellowish color, but it turns a rich red color as it matures. Many people eat them raw. Some use the seeds as dessert toppings and others press the seeds and pulp to make juice.

It is amazing the number of seeds in one fruit. The seeds can be taken from the inside of the fruit, dried on a paper towel, and then planted in moist potting soil. Sprinkle the seeds in a thin layer on top of the soil. Use your hands to press them slightly into the soil. Do not cover them with dirt because they need the sunlight in order to germinate. They must be watered daily until the sprouts come up. This will take about six weeks. They will only need to be watered when the soil feels dry after they have sprouted.

As we share with lost people the Word of God, seeds are sown in their heart. They come to know Jesus when these seeds sprout and they are freed from the bondage of sin. In the scripture, sin is referred to as darkness.

> In the beginning was the Word, and the Word was with God, and the Word was God. He was in the beginning with God. In Him was life, and the life was the light of men. And the light shines in the darkness, and the darkness did not comprehend it.
>
> John 1:1-2, 4-5 (NASB)

In his commentary on the Gospel of John, Warren Wiersbe mentions four things necessary for human beings to survive. They are light, air, water and food. Jesus Christ is all four of these.

Let's consider the fact that Jesus is light. "Then Jesus spoke to them again: "I am the light of the world. Anyone who follows Me will never walk in the darkness but will have the light of life" (John 8:12, HCSB). There is only one way people can be saved and that is by believing in Jesus. "Jesus told him, "I am the way, the truth, and the life. No one comes to the Father except through Me" (John 14:6, HCSB). When people come to know Jesus, they will never walk in darkness again. For new Christians to grow in the Lord, they must continually be exposed to the light, which is Jesus. They need to spend time studying the Bible so that they come to understand more about the characteristics of Jesus and how they are to imitate His life. "Therefore be imitators of God, as beloved children; and walk in love, just as Christ also loved you, and gave Himself up for us, an offering and a sacrifice to God as a fragrant aroma" (Ephesians 5:1-2, NASB).

The seeds from the pomegranate must be left uncovered in the soil in order that they can get the proper sunlight so the seeds will sprout. When new believers are exposed continually to the light of Jesus through the study of the scriptures, they will develop a strong root system in their spiritual life. Light is essential to the sprouting of the pomegranate seeds. An intimate relationship with Jesus, the light of the world, is essential to the growth of new born-again believers.

Appendix

Translations of the Bible used in the manuscript:

Amplified, Copyright 1987 by The Zondervan Corporation and the Lockman Foundation.

Holman Christian Standard Bible, Copyright 2004 by Homan Bible Publishers.

New American Standard Bible, Copyright 1985 by Holman Bible Publishers.

New King James Version, Copyright 1996 by Thomas Nelson, Inc.